# Anguished
# English

# Also by Richard Lederer

*Adventures of a Verbivore*
*Basic Verbal Skills* (with Phillip Burnham)
*The Bride of Anguished English*
*The Circus of Words*
*Comma Sense* (with John Shore)
*Crazy English*
*The Cunning Linguist*
*Fractured English*
*The Giant Book of Animal Jokes* (with James Ertner)
*Get Thee to a Punnery*
*Have a Punny Christmas*
*Literary Trivia* (with Michael Gilleland)
*A Man of My Words*
*The Miracle of Language*
*More Anguished English*
*The Play of Words*
*Pun & Games*
*Puns Spooken Here*
*The Revenge of Anguished English*
*Sleeping Dogs Don't Lay* (with Richard Dowis)
*The Word Circus*
*Word Play Crosswords, volumes 1 and 2* (with Gayle Dean)
*Word Wizard*
*The Write Way* (with Richard Dowis)

WITHDRAWN

# Anguished English

## An Anthology of Accidental Assaults upon the English Language

*by*
Richard Lederer

*Illustrations by*
Bill Thompson

HUNTINGTON CITY-TOWNSHIP
PUBLIC LIBRARY
200 W. Market Street
Huntington, IN 46750

10  09  08  07  06     5  4  3  2  1

Text © 1987, 1999, 2006 Richard Lederer
Illustrations © 1987, 1999, 2006 Bill Thompson

All rights reserved. No part of this book may be reproduced by any means whatsoever without written permission from the publisher, except brief portions quoted for purpose of review.

Published by Wyrick & Company
An imprint of Gibbs Smith, Publisher

P.O. Box 667
Layton, Utah 84041
Orders: 1.800.748.5439
www.gibbs-smith.com

Printed and bound in the U.S.A.

Library of Congress Cataloging-In-Publication Data
Lederer, Richard, 1938
   Anguished English.
ISBN 0-941711-03-X (cloth); ISBN 0-941711-04-8 (PB);
ISBN 0-941711-81-1 (Rev. PB)
   1. Errors Anecdotes, facetiae, satire, etc.
2. English language — Errors of usage — Anecdotes, facetiae, satire, etc.   I. Title
PN6231.E74L4   1987   420.207   8740532

# Contents

✳

# III
## STOP THE PRESSES!

# IV
## INSPIRED GIBBERISH

# V
## GRAMMAR GAFFES

# Introduction

Mark Twain once wrote, "Man is the only animal that blushes. Or needs to." He could have added, "The human being is the only animal that truly laughs. Or needs to."

We all need to laugh. Recent studies have proved that he or she who laughs lasts. Each year the evidence grows that ingesting humor does a body good. Norman Cousins, who used laughter to conquer a debilitating disease, writes in *Anatomy of an Illness*, "It has always seemed to me that hearty laughter is a way to jog internally without having to go outdoors."

"A good laugh and a long sleep are the two best cures," winks an Irish proverb. A belly-shaking guffaw stimulates the circulation, fills the lungs, colors the cheeks, energizes the respiratory system, relaxes muscle tension, adds endorphins and T-cells to the immune system, aerates the capillaries, stabilizes blood sugar levels, dulls pain and inflammation, provides superb aerobic exercise, tickles the funny bone—well, you get the idea.

In *Make 'Em Laugh*, Dr. William Fry explains, "When laughter gets to the point where it is called 'convulsive,' almost every muscle in the body is involved." May *Anguished English* split your sides, rock your ribs, detonate your stomach into a rolling boil, and convulse every muscle you own.

Granting all the healthful effects of hearty laughter, I feel compelled to issue a warning: Overdosing on *Anguished English* could be hazardous to your daily routine. I caringly and carefully suggest that you sip the book slowly, imbibing no more than a chapter or two at a single sitting.

A word about the authenticity of the bloopers you are about to read: To my knowledge, all the fluffs and flubs, goofs and gaffes, blunders, botches, boo-boos, and bloopers in this book are certified, genuine, and unretouched. None has been concocted by any professional humorist.

In *Anguished English*, I lay before you the ripest fruits of a lifetime of being a hunter-gatherer of word botching. If you are a super duper blooper snooper, please send your best specimens to me at richard.lederer@pobox.com.

RICHARD LEDERER
San Diego, California
www.verbivore.com

# I

# Schoolishness

*Wyatt Burp and Wild Bill Hiccup*

# Student Bloopers
# Win Pullet Surprises

✖

One of the fringe benefits of being an English or history teacher is receiving the occasional jewel of a student blooper in an essay or test paper. The original classroom blunder probably dates back to the day that some unsuspecting pupil first touched quill to parchment. Ever since, students have demonstrated a remarkable facility for mixing up words that possess similar sounds but entirely different meanings or for goofing up the simplest of facts.

The results range from the pathetic to the hilarious to the unintentionally insightful. The title of this chapter, for example, is based on a famous classroom faux pas: "In 1957, Eugene O'Neill won a Pullet Surprise." Other students have given bizarre twists to history by asserting that Wyatt Burp and Wild Bill Hiccup were two great western marshals and that the inhabitants of Moscow are called Mosquitoes.

Sometimes the humor issues from a confusion between two words. Working independently, students have written, "Having one wife is called monotony," "When a man has more than one wife, he is a pigamist," "A man who marries twice commits bigotry," and "Acrimony is what a man gives his divorced wife." While one student reminisced, "Each Thanksgiving it is a tradition for my family to shoot peasants," another observed, "In nineteenth century Russia, the pheasants led horrible lives." And, reversing a *g* and *q*, a young man once wrote, "When a boy and a girl are deeply in love, there is no quilt felt between them."

Side-splitting slips like these are collected by teachers throughout the world, who don't mind sharing a little humor while taking their jobs seriously. Many an inmate in the house of correction (of composition) knows the one attributed to William Lyon Phelps of Yale University, who allegedly found this sentence gleaming out of a student essay: "The girl tumbled down the stairs and lay prostitute at the bottom."

In the margin of the paper, the professor commented: "My dear sir, you must learn to distinguish between a fallen woman and one who has merely slipped."

From my own cullings and those of other

pedagogues, I offer my favorite student howlers, each a certifiably pure and priceless gem of fractured English worthy of a Pullet Surprise:

- A virgin forest is a place where the hand of man has never set foot.

- Although the patient had never been fatally ill before, he woke up dead.

- I expected to enjoy the film, but that was before I saw it.

- Arabs wear turbines on their heads.

- When there are no fresh vegetables, you can always get canned.

- It is bad manners to break your bread and roll in your soup.

- The problem with intersexual swimming is that the boys often outstrip the girls.

- Running is a unique experience, and I thank God for exposing me to the track team.

- A triangle which has an angle of 135 degrees is called an obscene triangle.

- The dog ran across the lawn, emitting whelps all the way.

- A virtuoso is a musician with real high morals.

- We had a longer holiday than usual this year because the school was closed for altercations.

Bloopers abound in all types of classrooms. Take these (please!) from English papers:

- The bowels are *a, e, i, o, u*, and sometimes *w* and *y*.

- A passive verb is when the subject is the sufferer, as in "I am loved."

- In *Great Expectations*, Miss Havisham puts herself into conclusion.

- The first scene I would like to analize occurs in *Heart of Darkness*.

- At the start of *The Grapes of Wrath*, Oklahoma has been hit by a dust bowl.

- At the end of *The Awakening*, Edna thinks only of herself. Her suicide is selfish because she leaves all who care about her behind.

- In *The Glass Menagerie*, Laura's leg keeps coming between her and other people.

- The death of Francis Macomber was a turning point in his life.

Students often revise history beyond recognition:

- The Gorgons had long snakes in their hair. They looked like women, only more horrible.

- Zwingli's followers all smashed their organs.

- Zanzibar is noted for its monkeys. The British governor lives there.

- The Puritans thought every event significant because it was a massage from God.

- The divine wind protected Japan by sinking the fleet of invading Mongrels.

- During the years 1933-38, there were domestic problems at home as well as abroad.

- The President of the United States, in having foreign affairs, has to have the consent of the Senate.

- The difference between a king and a president is that a king is the son of his father, but a president isn't.

And even the science and health classrooms are not immune from verbal schoolishness:

- To collect sulphur, hold a deacon over a flame in a test tube.

- $H_2O$ is hot water, and $CO_2$ is cold water.

- Three kinds of blood vessels are arteries, vanes, and caterpillars.

- A fossil is an extinct animal. The older it is, the more extinct it is.

- The human is more intelligent than the beast because the human brain has more convulsions.

- Artificial insemination is when the farmer does it to the cow and not the bull.

- To be a good nurse, you must be absolutely sterile.

- When you breathe, you inspire. When you do not breathe, you expire.

- Many women believe that an alcoholic binge will have no ill effects on the unborn fetus, but that is a large misconception.

Finally, I give you some special tour de farces in

which students offer penetrating glimpses into the obvious—and the not-so-obvious:

- Rural life is lived mostly in the country.

- Heredity means that if your grandfather didn't have any children, then your father probably wouldn't have any, and neither would you, probably.

- Last year many lives were caused by accidents.

- Abstinence is a good thing if practiced in moderation.

- The amount of education you have determines your loot in life.

- Necessity is the mother of convention.

All teachers who receive such bloopers tell themselves that the laughter is not at the students but at what they have written. After all, as one young scholar has written, "Adolescence is the stage between puberty and adultery."

# The World According to Student Bloopers

It is truly astounding what havoc students can wreak upon the chronicles of the human race. I have pasted together the following "history" of the world from genuine, certified, authentic student bloopers collected from teachers throughout the world, from eighth grade through college level.

Read carefully, and you will learn a lot.

The inhabitants of ancient Egypt were called mummies, and they all wrote in hydraulics. They lived in the Sarah Dessert, which they cultivated by irritation and over which they traveled by Camelot. The climate of the Sarah is such that the inhabitants have to live elsewhere, so certain areas of the dessert are cultivated by irrigation. Ancient Egyptian women wore a calasiris, a loose-fitting garment which started just below the breasts which hung to the floor.

The Bible is full of interesting caricatures. In the first book of the Bible, Guinness, Adam and Eve were created from an apple tree. One of their children, Cain, once asked, "Am I my brother's son?" Noah's wife was called Joan of Ark. Lot's wife was a pillar of salt by day and a ball of fire by night.

God asked Abraham to sacrifice Isaac on Mount Montezuma. Jacob, son of Isaac, stole his brother's birthmark. Jacob was a patriarch, who brought up his twelve sons to be patriarchs, but they did not take to it. One of Jacob's sons, Joseph, gave refuse to the Israelites.

Pharaoh forced the Hebrew slaves to make bread without straw. Moses led them to the Red Sea, where they made unleavened bread, which is bread without any ingredients. Afterward, Moses went up on Mount Cyanide to get the Ten Commandments, but he died before he ever got to Canada. David was a Hebrew king skilled at playing the liar. He fought with the Philatelists, a race of people who lived in Biblical times. Solomon, one of David's sons, had 300 wives and 700 porcupines.

The Greeks were a highly sculptured people, and without them we wouldn't have history. The Greeks invented three kinds of columns—Corinthian, Ironic, and Dork. They also created myths. A myth is a female moth. One myth says that the mother of Achilles dipped him in the river Stynx until he became intolerable. Achilles appears in the

*Iliad*, by Homer. Homer also wrote the *Oddity*, in which Penelope was the last hardship that Ulysses endured on his journey. Socrates was a famous Greek teacher who went around giving people advice. They killed him. Socrates died from an overdose of wedlock.

In the Olympic Games, Greeks ran races, jumped, hurled the biscuits, and threw the Java. The reward to the victor was a coral wreath. The government of Athens was democratic because people took the law into their own hands.

Eventually, the Romans came along and conquered the Geeks. History calls people Romans because they never stayed in one place for very long. At Roman banquets, the guests wore garlics in their hair. Julius Caesar extinguished himself on the battlefields of Gaul. The Ides of March murdered him because they thought he was going to be made king. Caesar expired with these immortal words upon his dying lips: "Eat you, Brutus!" Nero was a cruel tyranny who would torture his poor subjects by playing the fiddle to them.

The Romans were overrun by the ball bearings. Then came the Middle Ages, when everyone was middle aged. King Alfred conquered the Dames. King Arthur lived in the age of shivery, with brave knights on prancing horses and beautiful women.

King Harold mustarded his troops before the Battle of Hastings. Joan of Arc was burnt to a steak and cannonized by Bernard Shaw. People contracted the blue bonnet plague, which caused them to grow boobs on their necks. Magna Carta provided that no free man should be hanged twice for the same offence. People performed morality plays, about ghosts, goblins, and other mythical creatures.

In midevil times most of the people were alliterate. The greatest writer of the time was Chaucer, who wrote many poems and verses and also wrote literature. Another tale tells of William Tell, who shot an arrow through an apple while standing on his son's head.

The Renaissance was an age in which more individuals felt the value of their human being. Martin Luther was nailed to the church door at Wittenberg for selling papal indulgences. He died a horrible death, being excommunicated by a bull.

It was the sculptor Donatello's interest in the female nude that made him the father of the Renaissance. It was an age of great inventions and discoveries. Gutenberg invented the Bible and removable type. Sir Walter Raleigh discovered cigarettes and started smoking. And Sir Francis Drake circumcised the world with a 100-foot clipper.

The government of England was a limited

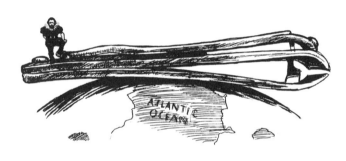

*Sir Francis Drake circumcised the world with a 100-foot clipper.*

mockery. Henry VIII found walking difficult because he had an abbess on his knee. Queen Elizabeth was the Virgin Queen. As a queen she was a success. When Elizabeth exposed herself before her troops, they all shouted, "Hurrah!" Then her navy went out and defeated the Spanish armadillo.

The greatest writer of the Renaissance was William Shakespeare. Shakespeare never made much money and is famous only because of his plays. He lived at Windsor with his merry wives, writing tragedies, comedies, and errors. In one of Shakespeare's famous plays, Hamlet rations out his situation by relieving himself in a long soliloquy. In another, Lady Macbeth tries to convince Macbeth to kill the king by attacking his manhood. Romeo and Juliet are an example of a heroic couplet.

Writing at the same time as Shakespeare was Miguel Cervantes. He wrote *Donkey Hoté*. The next great author was John Milton. Milton wrote *Paradise Lost*. Then his wife died and he wrote *Paradise Regained*.

During the Renaissance America began. Christopher Columbus was a great navigator who discovered America while cursing about the Atlantic. His ships were called the Nina, the Pintacolada, and the Santa Fe. Later the Pilgrims crossed the Ocean, and this is known as the Pill's

Grim Progress. When they landed at Plymouth Rock, they were greeted by the Indians, who came down the hill rolling their war hoops before them. Many of the Indian heroes were killed along with their cabooses, which proved very fatal to them. The winter of 1620 was a hard one for the settlers. Many people died and many babies were born. Captain John Smith was responsible for all this.

One of the causes of the Revolutionary War was the English put tacks on their tea. Also, the colonists would send their parcels through the post without stamps. Finally, the colonists won the war and no longer had to pay for taxis.

The United States was founded by four fathers. Delegates from the original thirteen states formed the Contented Congress. Thomas Jefferson, a Virgin, and Benjamin Franklin were two singers of the Declaration of Independence. Franklin had gone to Boston carrying all his clothes in his pocket and a loaf of bread under each arm. He invented electricity by rubbing cats backwards and declared, "A horse divided against itself cannot stand." Franklin died in 1790 and is still dead.

George Washington married Martha Curtis and in due time became the Father of Our Country. Then the Constitution of the United States was adopted to secure domestic hostility. Under the

*Franklin invented electricity by rubbing two cats backwards.*

Constitution the people enjoyed the right to keep bare arms.

Abraham Lincoln became America's greatest precedent. Lincoln's mother died in infancy, and he was born in a log cabin which he built with his very own hands. When Lincoln was president, he wore only a tall silk hat. He said, "In onion there is strength." Abraham Lincoln wrote the Gettysburg Address while traveling from Washington to Gettysburg on the back of an envelope.

On the night of April 14, 1865, Lincoln went to the theater and got shot in his seat by one of the actors in the moving picture show. The believed assinator was John Wilkes Booth, a supposingly insane actor. This ruined Booth's career.

Meanwhile in Europe, the Enlightenment was a reasonable time. Voltaire invented electricity and also wrote a book called *Candy*. Gravity was invented by Isaac Walton. It is chiefly noticeable in the autumn, when the apples are falling off the trees.

Johann Sebastian Bach wrote a lot of music and had a great many children. He kept an old spinster up in his attic on which he practiced every day. Bach was the most famous composer in the world, and so was Handel. Handel was half German, half Italian, and half English. He was very large. Bach died from

*When Lincoln was president, he wore only a tall silk hat.*

1750 to the present. Ludwig van Beethoven wrote music even though he was deaf. He was so deaf he wrote loud music. He took long walks in the forest even when everyone was calling for him. Beethoven expired in 1827 and later died for this.

France was in a very serious state. The French Revolution was accomplished before it happened. The Marseilles was the theme song of the French Revolution, and it catapulted into Napoleon. During the Napoleonic Wars, the crowned heads of Europe were trembling in their shoes. Then the Spanish gorillas came down from the hills and nipped at Napoleon's flanks. Napoleon became ill with bladder problems and was very tense and unrestrained. He wanted an heir to inherit his power, but since Josephine was a baroness, she couldn't bear children.

The sun never set on the British Empire because the British Empire is in the East and the sun sets in the West. Queen Victoria was the longest queen. She sat on a thorn for 63 years. Her reclining years and finally the end of her life were exemplatory of a great personality. Her death was the final event which ended her reign.

The nineteenth century was a time of many great inventions and thoughts. The invention of the steamboat caused a network of rivers to spring up.

Samuel Morse invented a code of telepathy. Louis Pasteur discovered a cure for rabbis. Charles Darwin was a naturalist who wrote the *Organ of the Species*, Madman Curie discovered Radio, and Karl Marx became one of the Marx brothers.

The First World War was caused by the assignation of the Arch-Duck by an anahist. In the Second World War Franklin Roosevelt put a stop to Hitler, who committed suicide in his bunk.

Martin Luther had a dream. He went to Washington and recited his Sermon on the Monument. Later, he nailed 96 Protestants in the Watergate Scandal, which ushered in a new error in the anals of human history.

# Excuses, Excuses

�֍

**M**y son is under the doctor's care and should not take P.E. today," wrote a parent. "Please execute him."

"Please excuse Mary for being absent," wrote another parent. "She was sick and I had her shot."

These drastic measures were inadvertently taken in notes written by parents to excuse their children's absences from school.

In all fairness to pupils throughout the land, I must point out that slaughtering the English language is a practice that is not limited only to students. An astonishing number of grownups blithely go about murdering the King's English without any inkling that they are committing a serious crime.

If you think that today's students aren't learning all they should, check out some of the writing miscreated by their moms and dads. The following are actual excuse notes received by teachers:

- Dear School: Please excuse John being absent on Jan. 28, 29, 30, 31, 32, and also 33.

- Please excuse Gloria from Jim today. She is administrating.

- Please excuse Roland from P.E. for a few days. Yesterday he fell out of a tree and misplaced his hip.

- John has been absent because he had two teeth taken off his face.

- Carlos was absent yesterday because he was playing football. He was hurt in the growing part.

- Mary could not come to school because she has been bothered by very close veins.

- Stanley had to miss some school. He had an attack of whooping cranes in his chest.

- Chris will not be in school cus he has an acre in his side.

- Please excuse Ray Friday from school. He has very loose vowels.

- Please excuse Pedro from being absent yesterday. He had ~~diahre dyrea direathe~~ the shits.

- Please excuse Tom for being absent yesterday. He had diarrhea and his boots leak.

- Irving was absent this morning because he missed his bust.

- Please excuse Jimmy for being. It was his father's fault.

- I kept Billie home because she had to go Christmas shopping because I don't know what size she wear.

- Please excuse Harriet for missing school yesterday. We forgot to get the Sunday paper off the porch, and when we found it Monday, we thought it was Sunday.

- Please excuse my son's tardiness. I forgot to wake him up and I did not find him till I started making the beds.

- Sally won't be in school a week from Friday. We have to attend a funeral.

- My daughter was absent yesterday because she was tired. She spent the weekend with the Marines.

- Please excuse Fred for being absent. He had a cold and could not breed well.

- Please excuse Mary from being absent yesterday. She was in bed with gramps.

- Gloria was absent yesterday as she was having a gangover.

- Please excuse Burma, she has been sick and under the doctor.

- Maryann was absent December 11-16, because she had a fever, sore throat, headache, and upset stomach. Her sister was also sick, fever and sore throat, her brother had a low grade fever and ached all over. I wasn't the best either, sore throat and fever. There must be the flu going around school, her father even got hot last night.

# II

## IT'S A
## BLUNDERFUL WORLD

# Disorder in the Court!

✖

Most language is spoken language, and most words, once they are uttered, vanish forever into the air. But such is not the case with language spoken during courtroom trials, for there exists an army of court reporters whose job it is to take down and preserve every statement made during the proceedings.

Court is now in session, and here are my favorite transquips, all recorded by America's keepers of the word:

Q. What is your brother-in-law's name?

A. Borofkin.

Q. What is his first name?

A. I can't remember.

Q. He's been your brother-in-law for 45 years, and you can't remember his first name?

A. No. I tell you I'm too excited. [Rising from

the witness chair and pointing to Mr. Borofkin]
Nathan, for God's sake, tell them your first name!

———

Q. Did you stay all night with this man in New
York?

A. I refuse to answer that question.

Q. Did you stay all night with this man in
Chicago?

A. I refuse to answer that question.

Q. Did you ever stay all night with this man in
Miami?

A. No.

———

Q. James stood back and shot Tommy Lee?

A. Yes.

Q. And then Tommy Lee pulled out his gun and
shot James in the fracas?

A. (After a hesitation) No sir, just above it.

———

Q. Doctor, did you say he was shot in the woods?

A. No, I said he was shot in the lumbar region.

———

Q. Now, Mrs. Johnson, how was your first marriage terminated?

A. By death.

Q. And by whose death was it terminated?

———

Q. What is your name?

A. Ernestine McDowell.

Q. And what is your marital status?

A. Fair.

———

Q. Are you married?

A. No, I'm divorced.

Q. What did your husband do before you divorced him?

A. A lot of things that I didn't know about.

———

Q. And who is this person you are speaking of?

A. My ex-widow said it.

———

Q. How did you happen to go to Dr. Cheney?

A. Well, a gal down the road had had several of her children by Dr. Cheney, and said he was really good.

———

Q. Do you know how far pregnant you are right now?

A. I will be three months November 8th.

Q. Apparently then, the date of conception was August 8th?

A. Yes.

Q. What were you and your husband doing at that time?

———

Q. Mrs. Smith, you do believe that you are emotionally unstable?

A. I used to be.

Q. How many times have you committed suicide?

A. Four times.

———

Q. Did he pick the dog up by the ears?

A. No.

Q. What was he doing with the dog's ears?

A. Picking them up in the air.

Q. Where was the dog at this time?

A. Attached to the ears.

———

Q. Doctor, how many autopsies have you performed on dead people?

A. All my autopsies have been on dead people.

———

Q. Were you acquainted with the decedent?

A. Yes, sir.

Q. Before or after he died?

———

Q. Officer, what led you to believe the defendant was under the influence?

A. Because he was argumentary, and he couldn't pronunciate his words.

———

Q. What happened then?

A. He told me, he says, "I have to kill you because you can identify me."

Q. Did he kill you?

A. No.

———

Q. Mrs. Jones, is your appearance this morning pursuant to a deposition notice which I sent to your attorney?

A. No. This is how I dress when I go to work.

———

Q. Have you ever been arrested?

A. Yes.

Q. What for?

A. Aggravating a female.

———

Q. You say you're innocent, yet five people swore they saw you steal a watch.

A. Your Honor, I can produce 500 people who didn't see me steal it.

———

JUDGE. Well, gentlemen of the jury, are you unanimous?

FOREMAN. Yes, your Honor, we're all alike-temporarily insane.

———

THE COURT. Now, as we begin, I must ask you to banish all present information and prejudice from your minds, if you have any.

———

Q. When he went, had you gone and had she, if she wanted to and were able, for the time being excluding all the restraints on her not to go also, would he have brought you, meaning you and she, with him to the station?

A. MR. BROOKS. Objection. That question should be taken out and shot.

———

Q. At the time you first saw Dr. McCarty, had you ever seen him prior to that time?

———

JUDGE. I rarely do so, but for whatever purpose it may serve, I will indicate for the record that I approached this case with a completely open mind.

———

Q. Did the lady standing in the driveway subsequently identify herself to you?

A. Yes, she did.

Q. Who did she say she was?

A. She said she was the owner of the dog's wife.

———

Q. I understand you're Bernie Davis's mother.

A. Yes.

Q. How long have you known him?

———

Q. Now I'm going to show you what has been marked as State's Exhibit No. 2 and ask if you recognize the picture.

A. John Fletcher.

Q. That's you?

A. Yes, sir.

Q. And you were present when that picture was taken, right?

———

Q. As an officer of the Dodge City Police Department, did you stop an automobile bearing Kansas license plates SCR446?

A. Yes, sir.

Q. Was the vehicle occupied at the time?

———

Q. Please state the location of your right foot immediately prior to impact.

A. Immediately before the impact, my right foot was located at the immediate end of my right leg.

———

Q. Have you ever beaten your wife?

A. No. I might slap her around a little, but I never beat her.

———

Q. Just what did you do to prevent the accident?

A. I closed my eyes and screamed as loud as I could.

———

Q. What can you tell us about the truthfulness and veracity of this defendant?

A. Oh, she'll tell you the truth. She said she was going to kill the son of a gun—and she did.

HUNTINGTON CITY-TOWNSHIP
PUBLIC LIBRARY
200 W. Market Street

———

Q. And another reason that you didn't want to go out there was because you feared for your life?

A. Yes, I did.

Q. Why?

A. That's a rowdy neighborhood, and there are very, very bad persons that will do bodily harm and seriously kill someone.

———

Q. Where were you on the bike at that time?

A. On the seat.

Q. I mean where is the street.

———

Before we recess, let's listen in on one last exchange involving a child:

Q. And lastly, Gary, all your responses must be oral, okay?

A. Oral.

Q. How old are you?

A. Oral.

# Accidental Bloopers

✿

Lord Chesterfield once wrote to a friend, "I'm sorry that I have written you a five-page letter; I didn't have time to write a one-page letter." Writing is hard work, and writing concisely is even more difficult.

Anyone who has ever had to fill out an insurance report on an auto accident knows how tricky it is to summarize the calamity in the small space usually allotted. The following statements are collected from insurance forms in which drivers were asked to explain their disasters in the fewest words possible.

This parade of narrative non sequiturs confirms that writing concisely, clearly, and objectively is no easy task and that even a mixed-up writer can be highly entertaining. In these cases, driving skills and writing abilities seem to go together:

- Coming home, I drove into the wrong house and collided with a tree I didn't have.

- A truck backed through my windshield and into my wife's face.

- In an attempt to kill a fly, I drove into a telephone pole.

- I had been learning to drive with power steering. I turned the wheel to what I thought was enough and found myself in a different direction going the opposite way.

- An invisible car came out of nowhere, struck my car, and vanished.

- I had been shopping for plants all day and was on my way home. As I reached an intersection, a hedge sprang up, obscuring my vision, and I did not see the other car.

- The gentleman behind me struck me on the backside. He then went to rest in a bush with just his rear end showing.

- The indirect cause of the accident was a little guy in a small car with a big mouth.

- The telephone pole was approaching fast. I was attempting to swerve out of its way when I struck my front end.

- As I approached the intersection, a stop sign suddenly appeared where no stop sign had ever appeared before. I was unable to stop in time to avoid the accident.

- I pulled away from the side of the road, glanced at my mother-in-law, and headed over the embankment.

- The guy was all over the road. I had to swerve a number of times before I hit him.

- A pedestrian hit me and went under my car.

- To avoid hitting the bumper of the car in front, I struck a pedestrian.

- I was sure the old fellow would never make it to the other side of the road when I struck him.

- I saw a slow-moving, sad faced old gentleman, as he bounced off the hood of my car.

- The pedestrian had no idea which direction to run, so I ran over him.

- The pedestrian ran for the pavement, but I got him.

- I was unable to stop in time, and my car crashed into the other vehicle. The driver and passengers then left immediately for a vacation with injuries.

- When I saw I could not avoid a collision, I stepped on the gas and crashed into the other car.

- My car was legally parked as I backed into the other vehicle.

- I was thrown from my car as it left the road. I was later found in a ditch by some stray cows.

- I told the police that I was not injured, but

on removing my hat, found that I had fractured my skull.

- The accident was entirely due to the road
bending.

- The accident was due to the other man's
narrowly missing me.

- The accident happened when the right front
door of a car came around the corner without giving a signal.

- The other car collided with mine without
giving warning of its intentions.

- No one was to blame for the accident, but it
never would have happened if the other
driver had been alert.

- She suddenly saw me, lost her head, and
we met.

- I misjudged a lady crossing the street.

- I heard a horn blow and was struck violently
in the back. Evidently a lady was trying to
pass me.

- One wheel went into the ditch. My foot jumped from brake to accelerator, leaped across the road to the other side, and jumped into the trunk of a tree.

- The accident occurred when I was attempting to bring my car out of a skid by steering it into the other vehicle.

- I had been driving for about 40 years, when I fell asleep at the wheel and had an accident.

- A cow wandered into my car. I was later informed that the unfortunate cow was half-witted.

- The other man changed his mind, and I had to run into him.

- I was backing my car out of the driveway in the usual manner, when it was struck by the other car in the same place it had been struck several times before.

- My car sustained no damage whatsoever, and the other car somewhat less.

- I was on my way to the doctor with rear end trouble when my universal joint gave way, causing me to have an accident.

# Wholly Holy Bloopers

✖

Let the word go forth that even the church is not immune from the havoc that an occasional howler can wreak. Throughout history numerous humorous fluffs and flubs have sneaked into various translations of the Bible.

A handsome edition of the Good Book published by Barker and Lucas in 1632 unfortunately omitted the little word *not* from the Seventh Commandment, making it read, "Thou shalt commit adultery." The careless printers of this edition, which became famous as the Adulterous Bible, were fined 300 pounds, effectively putting them out of business.

In 1716, thousands of copies of another Bible were printed before it was discovered that the command in John, "sin no more," had been printed as "sin on more," a letter reversal with considerable appeal to chronic transgressors. A year later, in an

Oxford edition of the Bible, a chapter heading for Luke appeared as "The Parable of the Vinegar."

A mix-up in gender in a 1923 version produced the stern admonition "A man may not marry his grandmother's wife," which the *New Yorker* called Neatest Trick of the Week.

The tradition of holy howlers popping up in religiously related documents continues un-dimmed. Witness the following sampling of bonafide bloopers culled from various church bulletins and orders of service:

- The ladies of the church have cast off clothing of every kind, and they can be seen in the church basement Friday afternoon.

- On Sunday a special collection will be taken to defray the expense of the new carpet. All those wishing to do something on the carpet will please come forward to get a piece of paper.

- Irving Benson and Jessie Carter were married on Oct. 24 in the church. So ends a friendship that began in school days.

- This week's saints include a French woman (Teresa, the Little Flower), a Swedish woman (Bridget), an Italian man (Francis of

*The ladies of the church have cast off clothing of every kind, and they can be seen in the church basement Friday afternoon.*

Assisi), a German man (Bruno), a Jewess from the Holy Land (Mary, God's Mother). They include single people and married people. Bridget was a wife and mother. Mary was a virgin and virgin mother. If they could do it, so can we.

- This afternoon there will be a meeting in the south and north end of the church. Children will be baptized at both ends.

- For those of you who have children and don't know it, we have a nursery downstairs.

- The Rev. Merriwether spoke briefly, much to the delight of the audience.

- The pastor will preach his farewell message, after which the choir will sing, "Break Forth Into Joy."

- This being Easter Sunday, we will ask Mrs. White to come forward and lay an egg on the altar.

- The choir will meet at the Larsen house for fun and sinning.

- Thursday at 5 P.M. there will be a meeting of the Little Mothers Club. All wishing to

*This being Easter Sunday, we will ask Mrs. White to come forward and lay an egg on the altar.*

become little mothers will please meet with the minister in the study.

· During the absence of our pastor, we enjoyed the rare privilege of hearing a good sermon when J.F. Stubbs supplied our pulpit.

· Will the ladies of the Willing Workers who have towels which belong to the kitchen please bring them to the church on Friday as we need them for supper?

- Wednesday, the Ladies Literary Society will meet. Mrs. Clark will sing, "Put Me in My Little Bed," accompanied by the pastor.

- Next Sunday Mrs. Vinson will be soloist for the morning service. The pastor will then speak on "It's a Terrible Experience."

- Due to the Rector's illness, Wednesday's healing services will be discontinued until further notice.

- Tuesday at 5 P.M. there will be an ice cream social. All ladies giving milk, please come early.

- The service will close with "Little Drops of Water." One of the men will start quietly, and the rest of the congregation will join in.

- Offertory: "Jesus Paid It All"

- Today—Christian Youth Fellowship House Sexuality Course, 1 p.m-8 P.M. Please park in the rear parking lot for this activity.

- The music for today's service was all composed by George Friedrich Handel in celebration of the 300th anniversary of his birth.

- Remember in prayer the many who are sick of our church and community.

On a church postcard:
- ❐ I have received Jesus Christ as my Lord and Saviour.
- ❐ I would like a personal call.

- The eighth-graders will be presenting Shakespeare's *Hamlet* in the church basement on Friday at 7 P.M. The congregation is invited to attend this tragedy.

- The concert held in Fellowship Hall was a great success. Special thanks are due to the minister's daughter, who labored the whole evening at the piano, which as usual fell upon her.

- 22 members were present at the church meeting held at the home of Mrs. Marsha Crutchfield last evening. Mrs. Crutchfield and Mrs. Rankin sang a duet, The Lord Knows Why.

- Smile at someone who is hard to love. Say, "hell" to someone who doesn't care much about you.

- A song fest was hell at the Methodist church Wednesday.

Today's Sermon:
  HOW MUCH CAN A MAN DRINK?
    with hymns from a full choir.

- Hymn 43: "Great God, what do I see here?"
  Preacher: The Rev. Horace Blodgett
  Hymn 47: "Hark! an awful voice is sounding"

- On a church bulletin during the minister's illness:
  GOD IS GOOD
    Dr. Hargreaves is better.

- Potluck supper: prayer and medication to follow.

- Don't let worry kill you off—let the church help.

Long may these bloopers live. Such unintentional levity brings lightness as well as light to many an otherwise dry church bulletin.

# Signs of the Times

On October 13, 1944, the *Durham* (N.C.) *Sun* reported that a Durhamite had been brought before a Judge Wilson in traffic court for having parked his car on a restricted street right in front of a sign that read "No Stoping."

Rather than pleading guilty, the defendant argued that the missing letter in the sign meant that he had not violated the letter of the law. Brandishing a Webster's dictionary, he noted that *stoping* means "extracting ore from a stope or, loosely, underground."

"Your Honor," said the man, "I am a law-abiding citizen, and I didn't extract any ore from the area of the sign. I move that the case be dismissed."

"No Stoping" is a blunderful example of the suspect sign and botched billboards that dot the American landscape. Here are some other signs that need to be re-signed:

- *At restaurant/gas stations throughout the nation:* Eat here and get gas.

- *At a Santa Fe gas station:* We will sell gasoline to anyone in a glass container.

- *In a New Hampshire jewelry store:* Ears pierced while you wait.

- *In a New York restaurant:* Customers who consider our waitresses uncivil ought to see the manager.

- *In a Michigan restaurant:* The early bird gets the worm! Special shoppers' luncheon before 11 A.M.

- *On a delicatessen wall:* Our best is none too good.

- *On the wall of a Baltimore estate:* Trespassers will be prosecuted to the full extent of the law.—Sisters of Mercy.

- *On a long-established New Mexico dry cleaning store:* Thirty-eight years on the same spot.

- *In a Los Angeles dance hall:* Good clean dancing every night but Sunday.

- *On a movie theater:* Children's matinee

today. Adults not admitted unless with child.

- *In a Florida maternity ward:* No children allowed.

- *In a New York drugstore:* We dispense with accuracy.

- *On a New York loft building:* Wanted: Woman to sew buttons on the fourth floor.

- *In a New Hampshire medical building:* Martin Diabetes Professional Ass.

- *In the offices of a loan company:* Ask about our plans for owning your home.

- *In a New York medical building:* Mental health prevention center.

- *In a toy department:* Five Santa Clauses. No waiting.

- *On a New York convalescent home:* For the sick and tired of the Episcopal church.

- *On a Maine shop:* Our motto is to give our customers the lowest possible prices and workmanship.

- *At a number of military bases:* Restricted to unauthorized personnel.

- *In a number of parking areas:* Violators will be enforced and Trespassers will be violated.

- *On a display of "I Love You Only" Valentine cards:* Now available in multi-packs.

- *In the window of a Kentucky appliance store:* Don't kill your wife. Let our washing machines do the dirty work.

- *In a funeral parlor:* Ask about our layaway plan.

- *On a window of a New Hampshire hamburger restaurant:* Yes, we are open. Sorry for the inconvenience.

- *In a clothing store:* Wonderful bargains for men with 16 and 17 necks.

- *In a Tacoma, Washington, men's clothing store:* 15 men's wool suits $10.00—They won't last an hour!

- *On an Indiana shopping mall marquee:* Archery tournament. Ears pierced.

- *In the bathrooms of a large apartment building:* When taking showers, please leave the bathroom door a jar. This will prevent the plaster from peeling.

- *Outside a country shop:* We buy junk and sell antiques.

- *On a North Carolina highway:*    EAT
                            3oo FEET

- *On an Ohio highway:* Drive Slower When Wet.

- *On a New Hampshire highway:* You are speeding when flashing.

- *On a Pennsylvania highway:* Drive carefully: Auto accidents kill most people from 15 to 19.

- *In downtown Boston:* Callahan Tunnel/No. End.

- *In the window of an Oregon general store:* Why go elsewhere to be cheated, when you can come here?

- *In a Massachusetts parking area reserved for bird-watchers:* Parking for birds only.

- *In a Maine restaurant:* Open seven days a week and weekends.

- *In a New Jersey restaurant:* Open 11 A.M. to 11 P.M. midnight.

- *In front of a New Hampshire restaurant:* Now serving live lobsters.

- *In front of a New Hampshire store:* Endurable floors.

- *On a radiator repair garage:* Best place to take a leak.

Before I sign off, I offer some poster and billboard messages containing the kind of goofy prose that laughs in the face of logic:

- *On a movie marquee:*    Now Playing:
                        ADAM AND EVE
                   With a cast of thousands!

- *In the vestry of a New England church:* Will the last person to leave please see that the perpetual light is extinguished.

- *In a Pennsylvania cemetery:* Persons are prohibited from picking flowers from any but their own graves.

- *On a roller coaster:* Watch your head.

- *On a New Hampshire road:*
                   Will build to suit
                   Emory A. Tuttle

- *On the grounds of a private school:* No trespassing without permission.

- *In a library:* Blotter paper will no longer be available until the public stops taking it away.

- *On a Tennessee highway:* Take notice: when this sign is under water, this road is impassable.

- Similarly, *in front of a New Hampshire car wash:* If you can't read this, it's time you wash your car.

And somewhere in England in an open field otherwise untouched by human presence is a sign that reads: "Do not throw stones at this sign."

# III
## STOP THE PRESSES!

# Two-Headed Headlines

One of comedian Will Rogers' favorite remarks was "All I know is what I read in the papers." For many busy people, all they know is what they read in the headlines. The bold messages entice readers to purchase copies from the news stands and, if there is time, to dive more deeply into a story.

Behind every newspaper headline lurks a newspaper deadline. The men and women who compose headlines work within pressing restrictions of time and space. They must compact large-size print into narrow column widths, and their brief messages must clearly state the theme of each story, keep words intact, be attractive to the eye, and catch the reader's attention. On top of that, each headline must be written in a fraction of the time thought humanly possible.

No wonder that, on occasion, editors get caught with their headlines down, and, exposed to as many as several million readers, the bold-face botch becomes a red-face result.

Some of the best two-headed headlines are those in which an inadvertent pun lifts the message from the blandly literal to the sublimely absurd:

GRANDMOTHER OF EIGHT
MAKES HOLE IN ONE

DEAF MUTE GETS NEW HEARING IN KILLING

DEFENDANT'S SPEECH ENDS
IN LONG SENTENCE

ASBESTOS SUIT PRESSED

DOCTOR TESTIFIES IN HORSE SUIT

COMPLAINTS ABOUT
NBA REFEREES
GROWING UGLY

POLICE BEGIN CAMPAIGN
TO RUN DOWN JAYWALKERS

*GRANDMOTHER OF EIGHT*
*MAKES HOLE IN ONE*

FLAMING TOILET SEAT CAUSES
EVACUATION AT HIGH SCHOOL

HOUSE PASSES GAS
TAX ONTO SENATE

POLICE DISCOVER CRACK IN AUSTRALIA

TUNA BITING OFF WASHINGTON COAST

STIFF OPPOSITION EXPECTED
TO CASKETLESS FUNERAL PLAN

MEN RECOMMEND MORE CLUBS FOR WIVES

MANY ANTIQUES SEEN AT D.A.R. MEETING

IKE SAYS NIXON CAN'T STAND PAT

TWO CONVICTS EVADE NOOSE; JURY HUNG

U.S. AUDIT FINDS FUNDS
FOR YOUTH MISSPENT

CHINESE APEMAN DATED

MAN HELD OVER GIANT L.A. BRUSH FIRE

TRAFFIC DEAD RISE SLOWLY

WILLIAM KELLY, 8₇, WAS FED SECRETARY

ALL-STARS TURN ON SPARSE CROWD

U.S. FOOD SERVICE
FEEDS THOUSANDS,
GROSSES MILLIONS

COLLEGIANS ARE TURNING TO VEGETABLES

MILK DRINKERS ARE TURNING TO POWDER

HALF-MILLION ITALIAN
WOMEN SEEN ON PILL

SAFETY EXPERTS SAY SCHOOL BUS
PASSENGERS SHOULD BE BELTED

———

SCIENTISTS TO HAVE FORD'S EAR

———

S. FLORIDA ILLEGAL ALIENS
CUT IN HALF BY NEW LAW

———

10 REVOLTING OFFICERS EXECUTED

———

QUARTER OF A MILLION CHINESE
LIVE ON WATER

———

DRUNK GETS NINE MONTHS IN VIOLIN CASE

———

COUNTY OFFICIALS TO TALK RUBBISH

———

JUDGE ACTS TO REOPEN THEATER

———

MAN HELD IN MIAMI AFTER SHOOTING BEE

———

SURVIVOR OF SIAMESE TWINS JOINS PARENTS

———

CARRIBEAN ISLANDS DRIFT TO LEFT

———

THUGS EAT THEN ROB PROPRIETOR

ROBBER HOLDS UP ALBERT'S HOSIERY

NEW HOUSING FOR ELDERLY NOT YET DEAD

TOWN TO DROP SCHOOL BUS
WHEN OVERPASS IS READY

FARMER BILL DIES IN HOUSE

KISSINGER ALLEGEDLY
FORGES MIDEAST PACT

GENETIC ENGINEERING SPLITS SCIENTISTS

IRAQUI HEAD SEEKS ARMS

SALESMAN SAYS HE LEFT
4 LARGE RINGS IN MALDEN BATHTUB

HERSHEY BARS PROTEST

MEAT HEAD FIGHTS HIKE IN MINIMUM PAY

*HERSHEY BARS PROTEST*

NEW AUTOS TO HIT 5 MILLION

When a newspaper goes out wearing the wrong banners, its messages can become unwittingly suggestive:

QUEEN MARY HAVING BOTTOM SCRAPED

IS THERE A RING OF DEBRIS
AROUND URANUS?

HENSHAW OFFERS RARE OPPORTUNITY
TO GOOSE HUNTERS

CONNIE TIED, NUDE
POLICEMAN TESTIFIES

WOMEN'S MOVEMENT CALLED
MORE BROAD-BASED

ANTIQUE STRIPPER TO DISPLAY
WARES AT STORE

STUD TIRES OUT

PROSTITUTES APPEAL TO POPE

CITY MAY IMPOSE MANDATORY TIME
FOR PROSTITUTION

SPLIT REARS IN FARMERS MOVEMENT

MRS. RYDELL'S BUST UNVEILED
AT NEARBY SCHOOL

JAIL GUARD PROBE IN PRISON SEX

GROVER MAN DRAWS PRISON TERM,
FINE FOR SEX ACTS

PANDA MATING FAILS;
VETERINARIAN TAKES OVER

KIDS' PAJAMAS TO BE REMOVED
BY WOOLWORTH

NUNS DROP SUIT, BISHOPS AGREE
TO AID THEM

PLANNED PARENTHOOD LOOKING
FOR VOLUNTEERS

N.J. JUDGE TO RULE ON NUDE BEACH

CHILD'S STOOL GREAT FOR USE IN GARDEN

IDAHO GROUP ORGANIZES
TO HELP SERVICE WIDOWS

COLUMNIST GETS UROLOGIST
IN TROUBLE WITH HIS PEERS

DR. RUTH TO TALK ABOUT SEX
WITH NEWSPAPER EDITORS

PASTOR AGHAST AT FIRST LADY SEX POSITION

MRS. CORSON'S SEAT UP FOR GRABS

SOVIET VIRGIN LANDS SHORT OF GOAL AGAIN

LOCAL MAN HAS LONGEST HORNS IN TEXAS

CAUSE OF AIDS FOUND—SCIENTISTS

STERILIZATION SOLVES PROBLEMS
FOR PETS, OWNERS

ORGAN FESTIVAL ENDS IN SMASHING CLIMAX

Sometimes the galley gaffe issues from a confusion in grammar:

BRITISH LEFT WAFFLES ON
FALKLAND ISLANDS

LUNG CANCER IN WOMEN MUSHROOMS

CITY PACTS FIGHT BOILS

EYE DROPS OFF SHELF

TEACHER STRIKES IDLE KIDS

REAGAN WINS ON BUDGET,
BUT MORE LIES AHEAD

SWAZI KING, 2 SONS POISON SUSPECTS

DEALERS WILL HEAR CAR TALK FRIDAY NOON

SQUAD HELPS DOG BITE VICTIM

MONDALE'S OFFENSIVE LOOKS HARD TO BEAT

AMERICAN SHIPS HEAD TO LIBYA

LAWYERS GIVE POOR FREE LEGAL ADVICE

LIFE MEANS CARING FOR
HOSPITAL DIRECTOR

HORNETS WILL ACCENT THROWING
GAME IN '81

SHOT OFF WOMAN'S LEG HELPS
NICKLAUS TO 66

MAN EATING PIRANHA
MISTAKENLY SOLD AS PET FISH

ENRAGED COW INJURES FARMER WITH AX

ADMITS SHOOTING HUSBAND
FROM STAND DURING TRIAL

LAWMEN FROM MEXICO BARBECUE GUESTS

PLANE TOO CLOSE TO GROUND,
CRASH PROBE TOLD

MINERS REFUSE TO WORK AFTER DEATH

JUVENILE COURT TO TRY
SHOOTING DEFENDANT

FUND SET UP FOR BEATING VICTIM'S KIN

STOLEN PAINTING FOUND BY TREE

FINE YOUNG MAN CONVICTED
OF MISDEMEANOR

HITLER, NAZI PAPERS FOUND IN ATTIC

SILENT TEAMSTER BOSS GETS
UNUSUAL PUNISHMENT, LAWYER

TWO SOVIET SHIPS COLLIDE, ONE DIES

2 SISTERS REUNITED AFTER 18 YEARS
IN CHECKOUT COUNTER

KILLER SENTENCED TO DIE
FOR SECOND TIME IN 10 YEARS

COMMUTER TAX ON NEW YORKERS
KILLED IN NEW JERSEY

Occasionally, a deformed headline takes on a meaning that is exactly the opposite of the one intended:

NEVER WITHHOLD HERPES INFECTION
FROM LOVED ONE

CANCER SOCIETY HONORS MARLBORO MAN

NICARAGUA SETS GOAL TO
WIPE OUT LITERACY

DRUNKEN DRIVERS PAID $1,000 IN '84

AUTOS KILLING 110 A DAY

LET'S RESOLVE TO DO BETTER
20-YEAR FRIENDSHIP ENDS AT ALTAR

And sometimes the headline illuminates the painfully obvious:

WAR DIMS HOPE FOR PEACE

IF STRIKE ISN'T SETTLED QUICKLY,
IT MAY LAST A WHILE

SMOKERS ARE PRODUCTIVE,
BUT DEATH CUTS EFFICIENCY

COLD WAVE LINKED TO TEMPERATURES

HALF OF U.S. HIGH SCHOOLS
REQUIRE SOME STUDY
FOR GRADUATION

CHILD'S DEATH RUINS COUPLE'S HOLIDAY

BLIND WOMAN GETS NEW KIDNEY
FROM DAD SHE HASN'T SEEN IN YEARS

———

SENSE FOUL PLAY IN DEATH
OF MAN FOUND BOUND AND HANGED

———

MAN IS FATALLY SLAIN

———

ENFIELD COUPLE SLAIN;
POLICE SUSPECT HOMICIDE

———

SOMETHING WENT WRONG
IN JET CRASH, EXPERT SAYS

———

DEATH CAUSES LONELINESS,
FEELINGS OF ISOLATION

# Galley Oops!

✖

A merica is a newspaper nation. Because our
country was the first great modern democracy,
the free press was born here.

Today there are about 1,650 newspapers printed
in the United States, and about one-fifth of the
newspapers printed around the globe are printed in
our land. Moreover, because of our extremely high
literacy rate (which you'd never guess from this
book), about 20 percent of the world's news readers
live here, even though we have only 6 or 7 percent
of the world's population.

When you think about it, the existence of a daily
newspaper is a miracle. After all, a newspaper is an
enormous product that must be manufactured from
scratch every day. Even more incredible is that millions of words pour forth from the nation's presses
each day, and almost every one of them is grammat-
ically accurate.

But, occasionally, under the pressure of constant deadlines, an editor will goof, and the results can be hilarious, ludicrous, or macabre. Let's have a look at some irrepressible gaffes from actual newspaper and magazine articles:

- The license fee for altered dogs with a certificate will be $3 and for pets owned by senior citizens who have not been altered the fee will be $1.50.

- The father was employed at the Seabrook nuclear power plant, and commuted for some months. Then the family moved to Seabrook, where they are happily living.

- This coming Sunday evening, the President and his wife will deliver a joint television address on the subject of drug abuse.

- The spacious home of Judge and Mrs. Clayton was the scene of a beautiful wedding last evening when their youngest daughter, Carol, was joined in holy deadlock by Mr. Fox.

- The accident occurred at Hillcrest Drive and Santa Barbara Avenue as the dead man was crossing the intersection.

- In Sunday's *Telegraph* Dorothy Harlen writes

about a teenage prostitute who refuses to change her way of life despite the pleas of her mother. For home delivery, phone 448-6200.

- Mr. Benjamin Porter visited the school yesterday and lectured on "Destructive Pests." A large number were present.

- Columbia, Tennessee, which calls itself the largest outdoor mule market in the world, held a mule parade yesterday headed by the Governor.

- A whimsical number titled "London Derriere" was played by Stein as his salute to St. Patrick's Day.

- Zimbabwe Rhodesian guerrilla leaders demanded Monday that a Commonwealth peacekeeping force of several thousand men—one with teeth—be sent to enforce a cease-fire in the war against their forces.

- A man was arrested on charges of disorderly conduct after he was found nude in a car at a hotel parking lot. A woman staying at the hotel said a man, wearing only a T-shirt, confronted her near her room. The woman told police she chased the man, but he escaped.

· The assembly passed and sent to the senate a bill requiring dog owners in New York City to clean up after their pets, in penalty of $100 fine. The bill also applies to Buffalo.

· Recent tests conducted by a zoologist prove that grasshoppers hear with their legs. In all cases the insects hopped when a tuning fork was sounded nearby. There was no reaction to this stimulus, however, when the insects' legs had been removed.

· Knicks Notes. Knicks open regular season on the road against Cleveland on October 28, then are at home the following night against Washington, during which time Senator Bill Bradley's uniform number 24 will be retired. Bradley will join former teammates Willis Reed, Dave DeBuschere and Walt Frazier in hanging from the Madison Square Garden rafters.

· What is more beautiful for the blonde to wear for formal dances than white tulle? My answer—and I am sure you will agree with me—is "Nothing."

- The attorney general's office said yesterday that an autopsy performed on the headless body of a man found in Mason failed to determine the cause of death.

- The bride-elect was showered with pieces of her chosen china.

- He called on the Kentucky legislature to clarify the state abortion statute to define whether it applied to pregnant women.

- Because the garden party was partly in observance of the Year of the Disabled, the Queen and her family moved among the guests in wheelchairs and on crutches and aluminum walkers.

- *Moby-Dick*, the great American classic by Herman Melville, will be seen again next week with veteran actor Victor Jory in the title role.

- Weight Watchers will meet Tuesday at 7 pm at the First Presbyterian Church. Please use the large double door at the side entrance.

- Patrick Murphy, a retired plumber from Pasadena, teaches fellow elderly persons how to be handymen and women.

Moby Dick, *the great American classic by Herman Melville, will be seen again next week with veteran actor Victor Jory in the title role.*

- Joining Wallace on stage were new School Committeewoman Elvira Pixie Palladino and Boston City Councilman Albert (Dapper) O'Neil, both active opponents of court-ordered busing and Wallace's wife.

- Hear Paul Lucas. The complete dope on the weather.

- Weather: Sunny with a few cloudy periods today and Thursday, which will be followed by Friday.

- Black Panther leader Huey Newton, terming the 1974 murder charge "strictly a fabrication," said yesterday he will testify at his trial on charges of killing a prostitute against his lawyer's advice.

- 7:30 P.M.—*PM Magazine.* Featured: Restaurants that will, for a small fee, bring you breakfast in bed and Lou Ferigno the Incredible Hulk.

- "Bodywatch," a new series, begins with a special at 9 tonight on channel 2. Tonight's program focuses on stress, exercise, nutrition and sex with Celtic forward Scott Wedman, Dr. Ruth Westheimer, and Dick Cavett.

- La Leche League will discuss breast feeding at two meetings—Tuesday in the West Side and Thursday in the East Side.

- Citizens of Santa Barbara County are faced with a tax rise. Most of the money raised would be used for five foot policemen.

- Gretzky won his sixth consecutive Hart Trophy as the NHL's Most Valuable Player, an unprecedented feat that tied him with Gordie Howe as a six-time winner.

- Mrs. Betty Larkin is poorly this spring. Her face is much missed in church, it being always there when she is able to be present.

- Ronald Reagan was accompanied on his tour by his friend Chuck Connors, television's "Rifleman," who plugged Reagan every chance he got.

- Since the disclosures about his fiances, the usually ebullient Representative has been unavailable to reporters.

- Osborne chased it around the back of the net, dug the puck off the sideboards, and fired a pass to Poddubny, who beat Buffalo goaltender Tom Barrasso between the legs.

- The summary of information contains totals of the number of students broken down by sex, marital status and age.

- With 23 ½ pints, the two ladies were high players in four tables of duplicate bridge.

- A well-known beauty expert says that beauty is not a question of age. It is making the best of one's good paints.

- The women included their husbands and children in their potluck suppers.

- Gene Autry is better after being kicked by a horse.

- One can peek in most any evening on this home-loving young actress and find her cuddled up in an easy chair with a good boob before a crackling log fire.

- The document had been hanging on the wall in town hall since 1948 but was removed two years ago when painters came and sat on the floor.

- Medical ethics are the choices we make based on our value system in moral considerations in the field of medicine. One example is youth in Asia. We have got the choice of letting a person live on a machine or pulling the plug. What's right?

· The Idaho State quarterback pissed 356 yards and guided his team to a 41–21 victory over Drake. Field condition was a contributing factor.

· The bride was wearing an old lace gown that fell to the floor as she came down the aisle.

· Migraines strike twice as many women as do men.

· The sewer expansion project is nearing completion, but city officials are holding their breath until it is officially finished.

· The ladies of the county medical society auxiliary plan to publish a cookbook. Part of the money will go to the Samaritan Hospital to purchase a stomach pump.

· His death leaves a void in the community which will be hard to replace.

· The ball struck him on the right temple and knocked him cold. He was taken to Sacred Heart Hospital where X-rays of his head showed nothing.

- The judge dismissed suits filed against a priest accused of sexually molesting four altar boys, the Orlando Diocese, and its bishop.

- A federal grand jury has accused three women identified by the IRS as topless go-go dancers of concealing their assets.

Even when a newspaper staff discovers that it has splattered egg on its pages, the clean-up operation can be embarrassingly messy, as witness these three so-called corrections:

- Our paper carried the notice last week that Mr. Oscar Hoffnagle is a defective on the police force. This was a typographical error. Mr. Hoffnagle is, of course, a detective on the police farce.

- Yesterday we mistakenly reported that a talk was given by a battle-scared hero. We apologize for the error. We obviously meant that the talk was given by a bottle-scarred hero.

- In a recent edition we referred to the chairman of Chrysler Corporation as Lee Iacooccoo. His real name is Lee Iacacca. The Gazette regrets the error.

# Addled Ads

✻

The average American consumer is bombarded with hundreds of commercial messages a day, and some experts claim that the average child sees and hears 100,000 pitches before being old enough to attend school. Sometimes it seems that, in these messages, both the sponsors and the advertising agencies have abandoned the struggle to communicate clearly, washing their hands of sense and meaning.

On a paper placemat in a Massachusetts restaurant appeared this advertising atrocity:

NEWBURY STREET COIFFURE
AFFORDABLE
*An Alternative to Looking Good*

After tittering and scratching our heads for a while, we can reconstruct what happened in the framing of this cacophonous come-on. Apparently, the good folks at Newbury Street Coiffure meant to proclaim that their affordable prices afforded an alternative for looking good. But what came out was the message "Come to us and we'll throw gunk on your hair and pull some of it out. And we'll charge you very little to do it!"

As the following classified classics will demonstrate, there are often more laughs on the advertising and classified pages than you can find in the cartoons and comic strips:

- Lost: small apricot poodle. Reward. Neutered. Like one of the family.

- A superb and inexpensive restaurant. Fine foods expertly served by waitresses in appetizing forms.

- Dinner Special—Turkey $2.35; Chicken or Beef $2.25; Children $2.00.

- For sale: antique desk suitable for lady with thick legs and large drawers.

- For sale: a quilted high chair that can be made into a table, pottie chair, rocking horse, refrigerator, spring coat, size 8 and fur collar.

- Four-poster bed, 101 years old. Perfect for antique lover.

- Now is your chance to have your ears

pierced and get an extra pair to take home, too!

- Wanted: 50 girls for stripping machine operators in factory.

- Wanted: Unmarried girls to pick fresh fruit and produce at night.

- We do not tear your clothing with machinery. We do it carefully by hand.

- No matter what your topcoat is made of, this miracle spray will make it really repellent.

- For Sale. Three canaries of undermined sex.

- For Sale—Eight puppies from a German Shepherd and an Alaskan Hussy.

- Creative daily specials, including select offerings of beef, foul, fresh vegetables, salads, quiche.

- 7 ounces of choice sirloin steak, boiled to your likeness and smothered with golden fried onion rings.

- Great Dames for sale.

- Have several very old dresses from grandmother in beautiful condition.

- Tired of cleaning yourself? Let me do it.

- 20 dozen bottles of excellent Old Tawny Port, sold to pay for charges, the owner having been lost sight of, and bottled by us last year.

- Dog for sale: eats anything and is fond of children.

- Vacation Special: have your home exterminated.

- If you think you've seen everything in Paris, visit the Pere Lachasis Cemetery. It boasts such immortals as Moliere, Jean de la Fontain, and Chopin.

- Mt. Kilimanjaro, the breathtaking backdrop for the Serena Lodge. Swim in the lovely pool while you drink it all in.

- The hotel has bowling alleys, tennis courts, comfortable beds, and other athletic facilities.

- Get rid of aunts: Zap does the job in 24 hours.

- Toaster. A gift that every member of the

family appreciates. Automatically bums toast.

- Sheer stockings. Designed for fancy dress, but so serviceable that lots of women wear nothing else.

- Stock up and save. Limit: one.

- Save regularly in our bank. You'll never reget it.

- We build bodies that last a lifetime.

- Offer expires December 31 or while supplies last.

- This is the model home for your future. It was panned by *Better Homes and Gardens.*

- For Sale—Diamonds $20; microscopes $15.

- For Rent: 6-room hated apartment.

- Man, honest. Will take anything.

- Wanted: chambermaid in rectory. Love in, $200 a month. References required.

- Wanted: Part-time married girls for soda fountain in sandwich shop.

- Man wanted to work in dynamite factory. Must be willing to travel.

- Used Cars: Why go elsewhere to be cheated? Come here first!

- Christmas tag-sale. Handmade gifts for the hard-to-find person.

- Modular Sofas. Only $299. For rest or fore play.

- Wanted: Hair-cutter. Excellent growth potential.

- Wanted. Man to take care of cow that does not smoke or drink.

- 3-year-old teacher needed for pre-school. Experience preferred.

- Our experienced Mom will care for your child. Fenced yard, meals, and smacks included.

- Our bikinis are exciting. They are simply the tops.

- Auto Repair Service. Free pick-up and delivery. Try us once, you'll never go any-where again.

Our Bikinis
are
Exciting
They are
simply
The Tops!

·See ladies blouses. 50% off!

·Holcross pullets. Starting to lay Betty Clayton, Granite 5–6204.

·Wanted: Preparer of food. Must be depend-able, like the food business, and be willing to get hands dirty.

·Illiterate? Write today for free help.

·Girl wanted to assist magician in cutting-off-head illusion. Blue Cross and salary.

·Wanted. Widower with school-age children requires person to assume general house-keeping duties. Must be capable of con-tributing to growth of family.

·Mixing bowl set designed to please a cook with round bottom for efficient beating.

·Mother's helper—peasant working conditions.

·Semi-Annual after Christmas Sale.

·And now, the Superstore—unequaled in size, unmatched in variety, unrivaled inconvenience.

- We will oil your sewing machine and adjust tension in your home for $1.00.

And these beauties from the radio:

- Ladies and gentlemen, now you can have a bikini for a ridiculous figure.

- Be with us again next Saturday at 10 P.M. for "High Fidelity," designed to help music lovers increase their reproduction.

- When you are thirsty, try 7-Up, the refreshing drink in the green bottle with the big 7 on it and *u-p* after.

- Tune in next week for another series of classical music programs with the Canadian Broadcorping Castration.

# IV

## INSPIRED GIBBERISH

# Lost in Translation

Someone at the United Nations once fed a common English saying into a translating computer. The machine was asked to translate the statement into Chinese, then into French, and finally back into English.

The adage chosen was "Out of sight, out of mind." What came back was "Invisible insane."

A similar computer was given the task of translating into Russian and then back into English the bromide "The spirit is willing, but the flesh is weak." The result was "The wine is good, but the meat is spoiled."

Why not? "Out of sight" does mean *invisible*, "out of mind" does mean *insane*, *spirit* does mean *wine*, and *flesh* does mean *meat*. Well, sort of.

We chuckle at such absurdly literal translations, but they remind us that few idioms can be mechanically translated word for word from one language to another.

At the climax of John F. Kennedy's impassioned speech in 1963 at the Berlin Wall, the President had wanted to say, *"Ich bin Berliner!"*—"I am a Berliner!"—since in German, words for nationalities are not preceded by articles. What Kennedy actually said was, *"Ich bin ein Berliner!"*—"I am a jelly doughnut!"

During a tour of Poland, President Jimmy Carter attempted to convey the message "I have a strong desire to know the Polish people." Through an inept translator the message emerged as "I desire the Polish people carnally."

When Pepsi-Cola invaded the huge Chinese market, the product's slogan, "Come alive with the Pepsi generation," was rendered (or should I say rent?) into Chinese as "Pepsi brings back your dead ancestors!"

While in Frankfurt (appropriately), I once asked a German storekeeper for a "heisser hund"—literally "a hot dog." He burst out laughing, as "heisser hund" in German suggests a dog in heat.

As people around the world have come to recognize and use English as the international lingua franca, they have begun adopting our language for the benefit of visitors. Or should I say adapting it, because much of the English abroad is infused with the spirits of Mrs. Malaprop, Desi Arnaz, Samuel

*Ich bin ein Berliner! (I am a jelly doughnut.)*

Goldwyn, Yogi Berra, Howard Cossell, and Archie Bunker.

Consider now my favorite examples of truly inspired gibberish collected (if you'll pardon the mixed metaphor) from the four corners of the globe:

- *In a Tokyo hotel:* Is forbitten to steal hotel towels please. If you are not person to do such thing is please not to read notis.

- *In another Japanese hotel room:* Please to bathe inside the tub.

- *In a Bucharest hotel lobby:* The lift is being fixed for the next day. During that time we regret that you will be unbearable.

- *In a Leipzig elevator:* Do not enter the lift backwards, and only when lit up.

- *In a Belgrade hotel elevator:* To move the cabin, push button for wishing floor. If the cabin should enter more persons, each one should press number of wishing floor. Driving is then going alphabetically by national order.

- *In a Paris hotel elevator:* Please leave your values at the front desk.

- *In a hotel in Athens:* Visitors are expected to complain at the office between the hours of 9 and 11 A.M. daily.

- *In a Yugoslavian hotel:* The flattening of underwear with pleasure is the job of the chambermaid.

- *In a Japanese hotel:* You are invited to take advantage of the chambermaid.

- *In the lobby of a Moscow hotel across from a Russian Orthodox monastery:* You are welcome to visit the cemetery where famous Russian and Soviet composers, artists, and writers are buried daily except Thursday.

- *In an Austrian hotel catering to skiers:* Not to perambulate the corridors in the hours of repose in the boots of ascension.

- *On the menu of a Swiss restaurant:* Our wines leave you nothing to hope for.

- *On the menu of a Polish hotel:* Salad a firm's own make; limpid red beet soup with cheesy dumplings in the form of a finger; roasted duck let loose; beef rashers beaten up in the country people's fashion.

- *In a Hong Kong supermarket:* For your con-

venience, we recommend courteous, efficient self-service.

- *Outside a Hong Kong tailor shop:* Ladies may
  have a fit upstairs.

- *In a Bangkok dry cleaner's:* Drop your
  trousers here for best results.

- *Outside a Paris dress shop:* Dresses for street
  walking.

- *In a Rhodes tailor shop:* Order your summers
  suit. Because is big rush we will execute customers in strict rotation.

- *Similarly, from the Soviet Weekly:* There will
  be a Moscow Exhibition of Arts by 15,000
  Soviet Republic painters and sculptors.
  These were executed over the past two
  years.

- *In an East African newspaper:* A new swimming pool is rapidly taking shape since the
  contractors have thrown in the bulk of their
  workers.

- *In a Vienna hotel:* In case of fire, do your
  utmost to alarm the hotel porter.

- *A sign posted in Germany's Black Forest:* It is

strictly forbidden on our black forest camping site that people of different sex, for instance, men and women, five together in one tent unless they are married with each other for that purpose.

· *In a Zurich hotel:* Because of the impropriety of entertaining guests of the opposite sex in the bedroom, it is suggested that the lobby be used for this purpose.

· *In an advertisement by a Hong Kong dentist:* Teeth extracted by the latest Methodists.

· *A translated sentence from a Russian chess book:* A lot of water has been passed under the bridge since this variation has been played.

· *In a Rome laundry:* Ladies, leave your clothes here and spend the afternoon having a good time.

· *In a Czechoslovakian tourist agency:* Take one of our horse-driven city tours—we guarantee no miscarriages.

· *Advertisement for donkey rides in Thailand:*

Would you like to ride on your own ass?

- *On the faucet in a Finnish washroom:* To stop the drip, turn cock to right.

- *In the window of a Swedish furrier:* Fur coats made for ladies from their own skin.

- *On the box of a clockwork toy made in Hong Kong:* Guaranteed to work throughout its useful life.

- *Detour sign in Kyushi, Japan:* Stop: Drive Sideways.

- *In a Swiss mountain inn:* Special today—no ice cream.

- *In a Bangkok temple:* It is forbidden to enter a woman even a foreigner if dressed as a man.

- *In a Tokyo bar:* Special cocktails for ladies with nuts.

- *In a Copenhagen airline ticket office:* We take your bags and send them in all directions.

- *On the door of a Moscow hotel room:* If this is

your first visit to the USSR, you are welcome to it.

- *In a Norwegian cocktail lounge:* Ladies are requested not to have children in the bar.

- *At a Budapest zoo:* Please do not feed the animals. If you have any suitable food, give it to the guard on duty.

- *In the office of a Roman doctor:* Specialist in women and other diseases.

- *In an Acapulco hotel:* The manager has personally passed all the water served here.

- *In a Tokyo shop:* Our nylons cost more than common, but you'll find they are best in the long run.

Finally, two charming sets of instructions from the land of the rising sun:

- *From a Japanese information booklet about using a hotel air conditioner.* Cooles and Heates: If you want just condition of warm in your room, please control yourself.

- *From the brochure of a car rental firm in Tokyo:* When passenger of foot heave in sight, tootle the horn. Trumpet him melodiously at first, but if he still obstacles your passage then tootle him with vigor.

All this global gabble is best summarized by two signs in a Majorcan shop entrance: "English well talking" and "Here speeching American."

# Modern-Day Malapropisms

During the early years of space exploration, NASA scientist Wernher von Braun gave many speeches on the wonders and promises of rocketry and space flight. After one of his talks, von Braun found himself clinking cocktail glasses with an adoring woman from the audience.

"Dr. von Braun," the woman gushed, "I just loved your speech, and I found it of absolutely infinitesimal value!"

"Well then," von Braun gulped, "I guess I'll have to publish it posthumously."

"Oh yes!" the woman came right back. "And the sooner the better!"

Long-time Chicago mayor Richard J. Daley was known for beheading the English language with such mutilations as "I resent your insinuendoes" and "We shall reach greater and greater platitudes of achievement." Mr. Daley's creative word choices must have been contagious because another

Chicago politician was heard to shout, "I don't want to cast asparagus at my opponent!"

When people misuse words in an illiterate but humorous manner, we call the result a malapropism (French, mal a propos—"not appropriate"). The term springs from the name of a character in Richard Sheridan's comedy *The Rivals*, written in 1775, and has come to stand for the kind of linguistic maladroitness exemplified in the statements above.

Mrs. Malaprop was an "old weather-beaten she-dragon" who took special pride in her use of the King's English: "Sure, if I reprehend anything in this world, it is the use of my oracular tongue and a nice derangement of epitaphs!" She meant, of course, that if she comprehended anything, it was the use of her oral tongue and a nice arrangement of epithets.

In Sheridan's play, Mrs. Malaprop urges her niece, who is "as headstrong as an allegory on the banks of the Nile," to "illiterate" a gentleman from her memory and to acquire a knowledge of the "contagious" countries.

It has been more than 200 years since Mrs. Malaprop first strode the stage, but time has not dulled our malpropensity for uttering malapropisms. As evidence of this insertion—oops! I mean assertion—I present my favorite modem examples of big word abusage:

- I am privileged to speak at this millstone in the history of this college.

- Medieval cathedrals were supported by flying buttocks.

- Beware of sexy women like those lymphomaniacs.

- They had to give one of the players artificial insemination.

- The mountain is named for the Rev. Starr King, who was an invertebrate climber and author of the book, "The White Hills."

- We can't be a pancreas to the whole world's problems.

- He's a wealthy typhoon.

- No phonographic pictures allowed.

- They call it P.M.S.—Pre-Minstrel Syndrome.

- He died interstate.

- His 90-year-old grandmother still has all her facilities.

*Beware of sexy woman like those lymphomaniacs.*

- They were singing without accompaniment. You know—Acapulco.

- I saw all those old testament houses.

- The first thing they do when a baby is born is to cut its biblical cord.

- His acting ran the gauntlet from A to Z.

- My daughter has a congenial hip disease.

- The referee penalized the team for unnecessary roughage.

- The Archbishop is interested in the economical movement.

- If Cartier had scored and we had gone on to win the game, all these questions today would have been irreverent.

- I suffer from a deviant septum.

- The police surrounded the building on three sides and threw an accordion around the block.

- You're in for a shrewd awakening.

- The young of the hoatzin, a curious fowl-like bird native to South America, are remarkable in having clawed fingers on their wings,

# E 'GADS, HER MINSTREL PERIOD IS STARTING

*They call it P.M.S.—Pre-Minstrel Syndrome.*

by means of which they are able to climb about trees like quadruplets.

- Still another faucet of Lamb's personality is revealed in his *Dream Children.*

- These imported trees are so profligate they are crowding out the more fragile native species.

- His mother got it all on film for prosperity.

- The marriage was consummated at the altar.

- Marriage was ordained for the procuration of children.

- He's a child progeny.

- Poe's romance with Mrs. Stanard was purely plutonic.

- The monks sang gregarious chants in honor of the Lord's annotated.

- They've decided to raise my benefits, and they're making it radioactive!

- Growing up the lattice work were pink and yellow concubines.

- Many Jews hang masseuses from their doors.

- She has unmedicated gall.

- It's a nice momentum of the occasion.

- In many states, murderers are put to death by electrolysis.

- At the university, three classes of professors compromise the teaching staff.

- The corporation has set up rules for the employees, and we expect you to live up to them sacrilegiously.

- That needs some thinking about. Let me go away and regurgitate for a couple of hours.

- Politically they were at locker-heads.

- My husband is a marvelous lover. He knows all my erroneous zones.

Now that you've become enarmored of mala-propisms, allow me to close my inquisition with the most pyrotechnical examples of the genre. The best malapropisms are those that leap across the chasm of absurdity and land on the side of truth. Sticking with French roots, we might call these bienapropisms.

For instance, the student who wrote, "The auto-mobile has had a beneficiary effect on the American family" illuminated reality more brightly than he or she could have imagined. The same goes for the creator of "There's so much pornographic rubbish in print it buggers the imagination. " Note how the following bienapropisms, manage to snatch truth from the jaws of absurdity:

- In Star Wars America has come up with the penultimate system of defense.

- This movie is not for the screamish.

- They've put her in an exhilarated class.

- We sold our house and moved into one of those pandemoniums.

- The defendant pleaded exterminating circumstances.

- I ate in a restaurant today where the food was abdominal.

- The cookbook is being compiled. Please submit your favorite recipe and a short anti-dote concerning it.

- It's a fragment of your imagination.

- Apartheid is a pigment of the imagination.

- The hills were worn down by eroticism.

- The incumbent mayor exhumed confidence before the polls closed.

- Certainly the pleasures of youth are great, but they are nothing compared to the pleasures of adultery.

- He sees things from an unusual vintage point.

- Most readers will find this scholarly book to be obtuse.

- He suffered from unrequired love.

- I didn't tell them who I was. I used a facetious name.

- In the early Sixties, we were strong and virulent.

- Caesar's wife must be beyond refute.

- Both movies were stinkers that Indiana Jones could sue for deformation of character.

- We have so emaciated our laws that the young hooligan is immune from punishment.

- The Americans really have a free press; it's incarcerated in their constitution.

- The specialist charged exuberant fees.

- Salary commiserates with experience.

- Don't tell them who sent it. I want to remain magnanimous.

- I have been a prostrate patient for many years.

- You have to be beautified before you become a saint.

- Life begins at contraception.

- She's been dwindling in the stock market.

- "The immediate impact was quite bombastic," recalled Dr. Luther L. Terry, the surgeon general responsible for the famous 387-page report [on the effects of cigarette smoking].

- I don't like swimming in that pond because it has too much of that green allergy.

- I wish someone would make a decision around here. I'm tired of just hanging around in libido.

- To be a leader, you have to develop a spear de corps.

- Senators are chosen as committee chairmen on the basis of senility.

# Mixed-Up Metaphors

✖

In an installment of the comic strip "Peanuts," Snoopy sits atop his doghouse typing away at a manuscript, "The curtain of night enveloped the fleeing lovers. Though fiery trails had threatened, oceans of longing had kept them together. Now a new icicle of terror stabbed at the embroidery of their existence."

Then Snoopy turns to the reader and says, "Joe Metaphor."

In his heavy-pawed attempt to create poetic-sounding metaphors, Snoopy has outrageously mixed fire with water and an icicle with embroidery.

Metaphors are so much a part of everyday speech and writing that it is all too easy to sew two or more figurative ideas together to create a Frankenstein Monster. Such mutants are called mixed metaphors, and all of us, in all walks of life, blithely sail along mixing metaphors. Oops, I just

*That's a horse of a different feather.*

mixed one myself by stitching together the figures of walking and sailing.

A U. S. senator created a new animal when he exclaimed, "That's a horse of a different feather."

President Richard Nixon's brother, Donald, rose to new linguistic lows when he said, "It is unfortunate that it [Watergate] happened, but people are using it as a political football to bury my brother." The same metaphoric football was even further deflated when a national newscaster announced that "the political football is now in the Polish government's court."

I've heard Boston-area telecasters tell us that "a deluge of fires have plagued Somerville," "I'm sticking my neck out on a limb," and "the Celtics were on the short end of an old fashioned blowout." Indeed, sportspeak is so laced with metaphors that sports luminaries often provide us with the craziest flights of verbal fancy on record. Here are two pearls worth their weight in gold:

From former Oakland Athletics owner Charles O. Finley: "You can't come in and rape a club just like that. I'm fighting to survive, but what they're doing with this side agreement of theirs is turning all the hawks and buzzards loose on Charles Finley. I'm bleeding like a stuck hog, and they're waiting for the old ticker to stop. That's when they'll swoop in and pluck me dry."

And from Lou Brock, the great St. Louis Cardinals outfielder: "I always felt I was a guy who had the ability to light the spark of enthusiasm which unlocked the hidden geysers of adrenalin that causes one to play to the summit of his ability."

And even author Ian Fleming managed to mangle a metaphor when he wrote in one of his James Bond books: "Bond's knees, the Achilles heel of all skiers, were beginning to ache."

Now, without batting an ear, I present more of my all-time favorite mutilated metaphors, each one guaranteed to kindle a gale of laughter. About half of the gaffes are culled from statements uttered by Capitol Hill politicians:

- I wouldn't be caught dead in that movie with a ten-foot pole.

- The sacred cows have come home to roost with a vengeance.

- Milwaukee is the golden egg that the rest of the state wants to milk.

- I haven't gotten my tax refund back yet, and I'm going to ask my councilman to pull some punches for me.

- She'll get it by hook or ladder.

- The bankers' pockets are bulging with the sweat of the honest working man.

- That's a very hard blow to swallow.

- These hemorrhoids are a real pain in the neck.

- The slowdown is accelerating.

- That snake in the grass is barking up the wrong tree.

- When we get to that bridge, we'll jump.

- Don't sit there like a sore thumb.

- At this advanced stage, the United States can fine tune the end game.

- The idea was hatched two years ago, but it didn't catch fire until two months ago, when the co-directors jumped in feet first, Since then, things have really been snowballing for the trio.

- Everyone whose ox has been gored is going to be squealing.

- It's time to swallow the bullet.

- It's time to grab the bull by the tail and look it in the eye.

- I think they're using an avalanche of P.R. to set us up for a wave of tax proposals.

- Mr. Speaker, I smell a rat; I see him forming in the air and darkening in the sky, but I'll nip him in the bud.

- You are out of your rocker.

- Flexibility is one of the cornerstones of program budgeting.

- The budget deficit is an albatross we carry on our back.

- I favor this irrigation bill in order that we may turn the barren hills of my state into fruitful valleys.

- The sword of Damocles is hanging over Pandora's Box.

- It's as easy as falling off a piece of cake.

- I'm not going to be side-tracked into a tangent.

- Here's the crutch of the matter.

- I was so surprised you could have knocked me over with a fender.

- Let dead dogs sleep.

- Stop beating a dead horse to death.

- She was a diva of such immense talent that, after hearing her perform, there was seldom a dry seat in the house.

- Water hazards on this tricky course have been the stumbling block for many a golfer.

- I'd like to have been an eardropper on the wall.

- The promotion was a real plum in his hat.

- It's difficult living in a bowl of fish.

- Regret to inform you that the hand that rocked the cradle has kicked the bucket.

- Even members of the press have gone out of their way to rub in the bitter pill.

- They are really riding a tiger by the tail.

- He's like a duck out of water.

- From now on, I'm watching everything you do with a fine-tuned comb.

- That guy's out to butter his own nest.

- I would not have gone in there over my dead body.

- Many cities and towns have community gardening programs that need a little more help to get off the ground.

- He threw a wet towel on the meeting.

- That was a low blow between the belt.

- The press bends overboard to be fair.

- If the Board had done its homework, it would not have jumped on this political bandwagon and dug itself a bottomless pit.

- We've got to be careful about getting too many cooks into this soup, or somebody's going to think there's dirty work behind the crossroads.

- We both had crewcuts, which made our ears stick out like sore thumbs.

- In our school, freshmen are on the lowest rungs of the totem pole.

- He's between a rock and the deep blue sea.

- He's going to hell in a handbag.

WE BOTH HAD CREWCUTS WHICH MADE OUR EARS STICK OUT LIKE SORE THUMBS

- Let's hope that Steve Carlton gets his curve ball straightened out.

- If Pete Rose brings the Reds in, they ought to bronze him and put him in cement.

- Let us nip this political monkey in the bud before it sticks to us like a leech.

- He was a very astute politician with both ears glued to the ground.

I do hope that you don't think I've been making a mountain out of a mole hole, but that's the whole kettle of fish in a nutshell.

# An Irish Bull Is Always Pregnant

It's time to throw some bull—not just any kind of bull, but an Irish bull. And while we're at it, let's throw a herd of Irish bulls.

What is an Irish bull? Some dismiss it as a silly blunder born on the Emerald Isle. Others more tellingly describe an Irish bull as a statement fueled by a delightful absurdity that sparks forth a memorable truth. When asked the difference between an Irish bull and any other kind of bull, Professor John Pentland Mahaffey of Dublin University replied, "An Irish bull is always pregnant," providing a definition that is itself an example of the form defined.

Irish politics, literature, and folklore are replete with pronouncements that jump to a confusion:

- An Irishman is never at peace except when he's fighting.

- An Irishman will die before letting himself be buried outside of Ireland.

- Your Hannar, I was sober enough to know I was dhroonk.

- Gentleman, it appears to be unanimous that we cannot agree.

- Half the lies our opponents tell about us are not true.

- God bless the Holy Trinity.

- Talk about thin! Well, you're thin, and I'm

thin, but he's as thin as the pair of us put together.

- May you never live to see your wife a widow.

- I can resist anything but temptation.

- Be sure to go to other people's funerals, or they won't go to yours.

- This piece is chock full of omissions.

- The cup of Ireland's misery has been over-flowing for centuries and is not yet half full.

- Ireland and England are like two sisters. I would have them embrace like one brother.

- He is the kind of opponent who would stab you in front of your face and then stab you in the chest when your back is turned.

- We should silence anyone who opposes the right to freedom of speech.

- A man cannot be in two places at once, unless he is a bird.

- I marvel at the strength of human weakness.

- With hindsight, we all have 50–50 vision.

- The cynics may point to the past, but we live in the future.

- Councilor Kelly complained that the new road from Carnock to Linthaugh had not yet got off the ground.

Any implications that the Irish have cornered the bull market are completely unwarranted. Some of the best specimens of taurine eloquence thrive far from the green fields of Ireland:

- There are known knowns. These are things that we know we know. There are known unknowns. That is to say, there are things that we know we don't know. But there are also unknown unknowns. There are things we don't know we don't know.—*Donald Rumsfeld*

- I think that gay marriages are something that should be between a man and a woman.—*Arnold Schwarzenegger*

- My vision is to make California the most diverse state on earth, and we have people from every planet on the earth in this state.—*Gray Davis*

- If Lincoln were alive today, he'd be turning over in his grave.—*Gerald Ford*

- The United States is the primary military power in the world. No one is second to us.—*Dan Quayle*

- I wish the Arabs and the Jews would settle their differences like Christian gentle-men.—*Arthur Balfour*

- The streets of Philadelphia are perfectly safe. It's only the people who make them unsafe.—*Frank Rizzo*

- Why that's the most unheard-of thing I've ever heard of.—*Joseph McCarthy*

- The Panama Canal belongs to us. We stole it fair and square.—*S. I. Hayakawa*

- You couldn't get me on Mars if it were the last place on earth.—*Erma Cohen*

- Please accept my resignation. I don't want to belong to any club that will have me as a member.—*Groucho Marx*

- If you live to the age of a hundred, you have it made because very few people die past the age of a hundred.—*George Burns*

- I'm not afraid to die. I just don't want to be there when it happens.—*Woody Allen*

- Cocaine isn't habit-forming. I should know; I've been using it for years.—*Talullah Bankhead*

- Live within your income, even if you have to borrow to do so.—*Josh Billings*

- Wagner's music is better than it sounds.—*Mark Twain*

- Thank God I'm still an atheist.—*Salvador Dali*

- If I had known I was going to live this long, I'd have taken better care of myself.—*centenarian Eubie Blake*

- You have no idea what a poor opinion I have of myself, and how little I deserve it.—*W.S. Gilbert*

- We must believe in free will. We have no choice.—*Isaac Bashevis Singer*

- I distinctly remember forgetting that.—*Clara Barton*

- Of course I can keep secrets. It's the people

I tell them to that can't keep them.—*Anthony Haden-Guest*

· Football is an incredible game. Sometimes it's so incredible, it's unbelievable.—*Tom Landry*

· All generalizations are bad.—*R. H. Grenier*

· Always be sincere, even when you have to fake it.—*Irene Peter*

· After the eighties, the nineties will make the fifties look like the sixties.—*Dennis Hopper*

The sagacious Hobbes, the insightful tiger in the late comic strip *Calvin and Hobbes*, once predicted that "We can eventually make language a complete impediment to everything." The tradition of tongue-tangled English is alive and well and still living in the Emerald Isle, the home of the Irish bull. When the freethinking Quentin Crisp told the people of northern Ireland that he was an atheist and proud of it, a woman in the audience stood up and asked, "Yes, but is it the God of the Catholics or the God of the Protestants in which you don't believe?"

# Goldwynisms And Berraisms

❋

Over the centuries, some lucky people have been granted a measure of immortality by having had their names transformed into common English words. One way to achieve such posthumous fame is to become so closely identified with an idea that your name becomes an *ism*.

Thus, the philosophers Plato and Karl Marx are enshrined in the words *Platonism* and *Marxism*, and the French soldier, Nicholas Chauvin, pursued his patriotism so zealously and excessively that his name is preserved in *chauvinism*.

The Rev. William Archibald Spooner occasionally and unintentionally interchanged sounds in his statements—"Is it kistomary to cuss the bride?" "You are occupewing my pie"—and we call such comic transpositions *spoonerisms*.

The life and writings of the Marquis de Sade extolled the pleasures of inflicting pain, and the fictional characters of novelist Leopold Sacher-

Masoch enjoyed receiving pain. Today the names of these two men live on in the words *sadism* and *masochism*. (As the time-worn story goes, the masochist says, "Beat me, beat me!" and the sadist sneers, "No.")

Two new *ism* words knocking at the covers of the dictionary are *Goldwynism* and *Berraism*. Samuel Goldwyn and Lawrence "Yogi" Berra are two American legends who have created such bizarre flights of linguistic fancy, such mind-boggling malapropisms, mixed metaphors, Irish bulls, memorable non-sequiturs, and intuitive wisdom, that their names may one day enter the dictionary as *ism* words.

Sam Goldwyn came to America from Poland and became a legendary Hollywood movie producer. Perhaps even more enduring than the memorable MGM pictures he made are his classic manglings of the English language, now known as Goldwynisms:

- A verbal contract isn't worth the paper it's written on.

- I'll give you a definite maybe.

- We're overpaying him, but he's worth it.

- I never liked you, and I always will.

- Include me out.

- For your information, I would like to ask a question.

- Don't talk to me while I'm interrupting.

- I may not always be right, but I'm never wrong.

- Anybody who goes to a psychiatrist ought to have his head examined.

- The scene is dull. Tell him to put more life into his dying.

- This book has too much plot and not enough story.

- Every director bites the hand that lays the golden egg.

- In two words: im-possible.

- It's more than magnificent—its mediocre.

- Tell me, how did you love my picture?

- A bachelor's life is no life for a single man.

- Go see it and see for yourself why you shouldn't see it.

- Yes, my wife's hands are very beautiful. I'm going to have a bust made of them.

- We have all passed a lot of water since then.

- It's spreading like wildflowers!

- You've got to take the bull by the teeth.

- This makes me so sore it gets my dandruff up.

- If I could drop dead right now, I'd be the happiest man alive!

- When I want your opinion, I'll give it to you.

- I had a monumental idea last night, but I didn't like it.

- I never put on a pair of shoes until I've worn them five years.

- Color television! Bah, I won't believe it until I see it in black and white.

- We want a story that starts out with an earthquake and works its way up to a climax.

- I read part of it all the way through.

- Let's have some new clichés.

- Look how I developed Jon Hall. He's a better leading man than Robert Taylor will ever be—some day.

- Going to call him William? What kind of a name is that? Every Tom, Dick, and Harry is called William.

- We'd do anything for each other. We'd even cut each other's throats for each other.

- Our comedies are not to be laughed at.

- This new atom bomb is dynamite.

- Referring to *The Best Years of Our Lives:* I don't care if it doesn't make a nickel. I just want every man, woman, and child in America to see it.

- Goldwynisms! Don't talk to me about Goldwynisms, f'Chrissake. You want to hear some Goldwynisms go talk to Jesse Lasky!

As good as Goldwyn is Yogi Berra. Posterity may best remember the great Yankee catcher for the linguistic screwballs he has pitched over the years.

Many observers feel that Berra learned to mutilate the English language so creatively from his manager, Professor Casey Stengel, to whom is attributed such beauties as, "A lot of people my age are dead at the present time" and "Good hitting always stops good pitching, and vice versa." Apparently, Berra learned his lessons well, as demonstrated by the following classic Berraisms, also known as Yogi-isms. As Joe Garagiola sagely observes, "He says things funny. He says things that are a split second off the hinges."

- Sometimes you can observe a lot by watching.

- It ain't over till it's over.

- No wonder nobody comes here—it's too crowded.

- If the people don't want to come out to the park, nobody's gonna stop 'em.

- There are some people who, if they don't already know, you can't tell 'em.

- A nickel ain't worth a dime anymore.

- Even Napoleon had his Watergate.

- I want to thank all the people who made this night necessary.

- Half the lies they tell me aren't true.

Sometimes you can observe a lot by watching.

- If you can't imitate him, don't copy him.

- *Mickey Mantle:* "What time is it?" *Berra:* "You mean right now?"

- On why it's so tough to play left field in Yankee Stadium: "Because it gets late early."

- Ordering sweaters: "That's the kind I want. I want one in Navy blue and one in Navy brown."

- On receiving a check made out to "Bearer": "How could you spell my name like that?"

A story makes the rounds about the time that a waitress served Yogi a pizza and asked him if he wanted it cut into four slices or eight. "Better make it four," Yogi replied. "I don't think I can eat eight pieces."

Such a creative approach to mathematics marks two other beguiling Berraisms: "Why don't you pair 'em up in threes" and "Ninety-nine percent of this game is half mental."

Even if Yogi Berra's name doesn't make it into the dictionary, his engaging turns of phrase may live on through his son Dale. When the younger Berra was playing shortstop for the Pittsburgh Pirates, he was asked to compare himself with his father. His answer: "Our similarities are different."

# V
## GRAMMAR GAFFES

# Mangling Modifiers

✳

While grading a student essay on John Steinbeck's *The Grapes of Wrath*, I was startled to read this sentence: "Having killed a man and served four years in prison, I feel that Tom Joad is ripe to get into trouble."

Who had killed and done time—the student or Tom Joad?

Later in the same book report, the student explored the ending of the novel, in which Rose of Sharon Joad, having lost a still-born baby, offers her milk-laden breast to a starving migrant worker for nourishment. Steinbeck's closing sentence reads: "She looked up and across the barn, and her lips came together and smiled mysteriously." Here's what my student wrote: "Rose of Sharon now starts to reach out to others, and the book closes with her feeding a starving man, smiling mysteriously."

Ever since, the look on that fellow's face has remained in my mind's eye.

My student's two botched sentences are superb examples of the scalding water writers can get themselves into when they misplace a modifier. Many of the most amusing grammatical errors occur where ambiguous phrases and clauses end up in the wrong part of a sentence. Here is an array of adult—and adulterated—examples:

- Yoko Ono will talk about her husband, John Lennon, who was killed in an interview with Barbara Walters.

- After years of being lost under a pile of dust, Chester D. Thatcher III found all the old records of the Bangor Lions Club at the Bangor House.

- [Edwin] Newman, author of two Book-of-the Month Club books on the abuse of language, hinted in a speech to nearly 1,300 persons in the Memorial Union Theater that efforts to improve language may be the result of attacks on pompous, weird language such as his.

- Bound, gagged, and trussed up nude in a denim bag with plugs in her ears and tape over her eyes, Cleveland teacher Brenda P. Noonan told yesterday how she was kidnapped to Florida without knowing where she was going or why.

- Please take time to look over the brochure that is enclosed with your family.

- I wish to express my thanks to the Post Office for the great, kind service they give and for the patience they have with little old ladies in mailing packages.

- Plunging 1,000 feet into the gorge, we saw Yosemite Falls.

- CALF BORN TO FARMER WITH TWO HEADS

- CHURCHILL LEAVES WIFE LEANING ON PLANE

- BILL TO CURB PORNOGRAPHY SUBMITTED BY MAYOR BEAME

- Some sources said shortly after his death Mao Tse Tung had expressed a wish that his body be cremated.

- Two cars were reported stolen by the Groveton police yesterday.

- One couldn't help but be aware of the stallion Royal Rick sitting in the stands the last couple of nights.

- As a baboon who grew up wild in the jungle, I realized that Wiki had special nutritional needs.

- In 1979, he bought majority control of the company's stock, along with his mother.

- He rode his horse across Highway 12 and up and down the sidewalk in front of the saloon a good half hour before deputies arrived, shouting obscenities and being obnoxious.

- Last week Toronto policemen buried one of their own—a 22-year-old constable shot with his own revolver in a solemn display of police solidarity rarely seen in Canada.

- Locked in a vault for 50 years, the owner of the jewels has decided to sell them.

- Breaking into the window of the girls' dormitory, the dean of men surprised 10 members of the football team.

- The police said Barth's 1981 Toyota traveled down the shoulder for almost 1,000 feet and

DO NOT SIT IN CHAIR WITHOUT BEING FULLY ASSEMBLED

then hit a utility pole going about 45 miles an hour.

- The patient was referred to a psychiatrist with a severe emotional problem.

- Do not sit in chair without being fully assembled.

- A former scout leader will plead guilty to two counts of sexually assaulting two boys in a New Hampshire court.

- Found guilty on eight counts, Duchess County Judge Robert F. Howard sentenced Groman to six months in prison.

- She died in the home in which she was born at the age of 88.

- A 30-year-old St. Petersburg man was found murdered by his parents in his home late Saturday.

- Pele soaked an ankle he injured in an ice bucket.

- Washed from a layer of mudstone estimated to be more than 3 million years old, a young American paleoanthropologist has found several leg bones and a skull fragment.

- Amy Carter was among more than 100 Americans returning from a 10-day tour of the Soviet Union during the weekend.

- The judge sentenced the killer to die in the electric chair for the second time.

- Farmhand Joe Mobbs hoists a cow injured while giving birth to its feet.

- Here are some suggestions for handling obscene phone calls from New England Telephone Company.

- When a small boy, a girl is of little interest.

- Berra had driven over with his wife, Carmen, from their home in a Mercedes for the softball game.

- No one was injured in the blast, which was attributed to a buildup of gas by one town official.

# References Wanted

✻

Croesus, the last king of Lydia and the fellow we'd all like to be richer than, decided in 546 B.C. to make war on Persia. Being a careful man, Croesus sought advice from the oracle at Delphi. Should he invade Persia, or shouldn't he?

According to legend, the oracle answered, "If you cross the river Halys, you will destroy a mighty empire."

Croesus interpreted the sentence as a good omen and proceeded to attack Persia. But after many setbacks, the king was taken prisoner at Sardis.

The oracle had been right. By waging war on Persia, Croesus did destroy a mighty empire—his own.

King Croesus was a victim of an ambiguous reference. In the oracle's prophecy, the phrase "a mighty empire" could have referred either to Lydia or to Persia. Because Croesus failed to analyze the grammar of the sentence, his kingdom of Lydia ceased to exist.

Most reference problems are caused by the ambiguous use of pronouns:

- When Lady Caruthers smashed the traditional bottle of champagne against the hull of the giant oil tanker, she slipped down the runway, gained speed, rocketed into the water with a gigantic spray, and continued unchecked toward Prince's Island.

- Guilt, vengeance, and bitterness can be emotionally destructive to you and your children. You must get rid of them.

In the first sentence, who or what slid into the water—Lady Caruthers or the oil tanker? In the second example, is it guilt, vengeance, and bitterness or children that must be gotten rid of?

To show what happens when writers fail to pay attention to their pronouns and antecedents, I refer you to my favorite reference errors:

- After Governor Baldwin watched the lion perform, he was taken to Main Street and fed 25 pounds of raw meat in front of the Cross Keys Theater.

- Andie MacDowell, until now a leading model, makes her screen debut as the American ward of Lord Greystoke who falls in love with Tarzan.

- Anti-nuclear protestors released five cockroaches inside the White House Friday, and these were arrested when they left and blocked a security gate.

- The driver had a narrow escape, as a broken board penetrated his cabin and just missed his head. This had to be removed before he could be released.

- Great care must always be exercised in tethering horses to trees as they are apt to bark.

- A fortune cookie message: You have many personal talents that are attractive to others, so be sure to use them.

- Two cycles belonging to girls that had been left leaning against lamp-posts were badly damaged.

- Although her mother was in it, thieves stole a suitcase containing jewelry and clothing from the car of Mrs. Vanya Koskis yesterday.

*Although her mother was in it, thieves stole a suitcase containing jewelry and clothing from the car of Mrs. Vanya Koskis yesterday.*

- My mother wants to have the dog's tail operated on again, and if it doesn't heal this time, she'll have to be put away.

- Jerry Remy then hit an RBI single off Haas's leg, which rolled into right field.

- About two years ago, a wart appeared on my left hand, which I wanted removed.

- According to the report, a vehicle apparently ran off Ketch Road and struck the mailbox as it attempted to get back on the roadway.

- Two armed men forced their way into the mobile home of Lucille Cornell, taking Cornell and her sister hostage as they filled a van with antiques and other valuables.

- On the floor above him lived a redheaded instructor in physical education, whose muscular calves he admired when they nodded to each other by the mailbox.

- Confused by the noise of traffic, a bull that was probably experiencing its first taste of city life got mixed up with vehicles in Ellsworth Avenue and was struck by a street car. It was so badly injured that Patrolman Milton Elliman ended his life with a bullet.

- Do not park your car at the taxi stand or it will be towed away.

- "He's the horse of a lifetime," said trainer Packy Lawrence. He'll retire after today's race and be shipped to Kentucky, where he'll begin a career at stud.

- The French government is preparing commercials encouraging the use of condoms that are blunt enough to shock even liberal Americans.

- People who use birth control methods that smoke a lot are in danger of having retarded children.

Perhaps my favorite favorite is this classic from the annual report of a famous New England boarding school: "Where do the girls live? Our answer has been simplicity itself: assign girls to regular dormitories, thus removing them from use by boys."

# Laffing at Mispellings

✤

The English language is the most widely spoken in the history of our planet. The English language boasts the largest of all vocabularies and one of the most impressive bodies of literature.

But let's face it. The English language is a killer to spell correctly.

In *The Devil's Dictionary*, Ambrose Bierce defines orthography as "the science of spelling by the eye instead of the ear. Advocated with more heat than light by the outmates of every asylum for the insane." J. Donald Adams adds: "It is wildly erratic and almost wholly without logic. One needs the eye of a hawk, the ear of a dog, and the memory of an elephant to make headway against its confusions and inconsistencies." Mario Pei sums up the chaos this way: "English spelling is the world's most awesome mess."

No wonder, then, that many students have succumbed to the pitfalls of English spelling by executing spectacular pratfalls in their essays and test papers.

Decades ago, Carl Cochran, retired Professor of English at Colby Sawyer College in New Hampshire, taught at Shady Side Academy in Pittsburgh. He received a composition in which one of his students described his summer adventures in Venezuela, where he had worked for Gulf Oil Company. One error kept appearing throughout the paper. The student consistently misspelled the word *burro* as *burrow.* At the end of the essay, Professor Cochran wrote: "My dear sir: It is apparent to me from your spelling that you do not know your ass from a hole in the ground."

Other classic student spellos include:

- To celebrate at feasts, the inhabitants of old England sometimes cut the head off the biggest bore and carried it around on a platter.

- Floods from the Mississippi may be prevented by putting big dames in the river.

- Geometry teaches us to bisex angels.

- They gave William IV a lovely funeral. It took six men to carry the beer.

- On Thanksgiving morning we could smell the foul cooking.

- My uncle suffers from sick as hell anemia.

- I am in the mists of choosing colleges.

- The doctor told me to take it easy until the stitches were out and that there would be a permanent scare.

- In Pittsburgh they manufacture iron and steal.

- Every morning my father takes exercises to strengthen his abominable muscles.

- Many people believe he was a Satin worshipper.

- During peek season the beach is covered with hundreds of bikini-clad beauties.

- After consuming my mother's vitals, I went happily to bed.

- Most teachers could careless about the personal problems of their students.

- The pistol of a flower is its only protection against insects.

- They were sweathearts through high school.

- I know people who have found dishes and tools and bowels from the Indians.

- Vestal virgins were pure and chased.

- I worry about testes all week.

- During the Cavaleer age every lady had a night.

Writing about literature seems to bring out the best of orthographic atrocities:

- Defoe wrote simply and sometimes crudly.

- Austen deals with the concept of breading and ill breading in her work.

- Thomas Gray wrote the Alergy in a Country Churchyard.

- Dickens spent his youth in prison because his father's celery was cut off.

- Poe was kicked out of West Point for gamboling.

- *The Scarlet Letter* griped me intensely.

- Whitman wrote much illiteration and com-packed verse. He often wrote long and rum-bling fines.

· This book belongs in the anals of English literature.

The vagaries of English spelling continue to plague Americans long after they leave school. Signs of miraculous orthography appear everywhere:

· Drop your ballet in the ballet box.

· Please leave your umbrella and goulashes here.

· No bear feet allowed.

· Due to repairs to the air-conditioning system, offices will be very humid for the next three days. Please bare with us.

· Our menu is guaranteed to wet your appetite.

· Our sauce compliments our salad.

· Full coarse meals.

- Carats, 2 for 39 cents.

- Today's special: barely soup.

And the spelling demons continue to depress the nation's presses:

- Governor Sununu gave the president a sweater crotched by Ellen Garrison.

- Grace Varney's voice broke with emotion as she clutched her toe-headed daughter as her son clung to her side.

- The directors of the Starcross Corporation are planning a gala reception to show their appreciation of the outgoing Chairman of the Bored.

- To win in this league, you've got to knock your opponent down and run with wreckless abandon.

- At that point, the vessel will be secured and slowly pulled by wire, rope, and wench.

- Alice B. Toklas and Gertrude Stein were both American ex-patriots.

- She had a seizure—her third one—and she fell and went unconscious. She was in a comma, and she never woke up.

- For Lederer, teaching, writing, and public speaking are all a seamless hole.

- Concealing those aging fines with a rye smile, Cliff (Bill Cosby) models a party hat preparing for a Huxtable family get-together marking his 50th birthday.

- Merlin Olsen is the most inciteful of sportscasters.

- Koch called individual conservation the single most important faucet of the anti-drought program.

- Educating Today's Women
  For Tomorrow
  Wither the Curriculum?

- *Demon* is a nasty little film about the dead coming back and reeking havoc on the living.

The spelling demons love to come and live in headlines:

- MAN ARRESTED FOR
  POSSESSION OF HEROINE

- PANEL AGREE TO MUCH
  SEX ON TELEVISION

- SLUM RAISING PLAN ASSAILED

- REAGAN GOES FOR
  JUGGLER IN MIDWEST

- COAST GUARD RESCUES TWO VESSELS
  AS STORM POMMELS GEORGIA COAST

These especially embarrassing spellos have
caused many an editor to have a spell:

- Correction: Ernest and Hilda Grunzweig's
  names were mispelled in yesterday's
  edition.

- NEWSPAPER TO RECIEVE 7 AWARDS

- Accuratley Yours: Professional word pro-
  cessing company. Open 24 hours each day.

- Writing clearly is essential to today's high
  tech, information-oriented society. This
  course assures you have a basic understand-
  ing of grammer and punctuation.

- Editors and Proff Readers—Must be good in
  spelling and grammar.

- LITERARCY WEEK OBSERVED.

- On the whole, the standard of work in the

anthology is high, and despite sloopy proof-reading, the book makes pleasant reading.

· Our Spellwriter has the power to check spelling of words within a document in as many as eight different languages. And this is only the tip of the iceburg.

· 6 room cottage nestled amongst beautiful trees. Mint condition, nicely furnished, antiques, carpeting, and assessible all year round.

And perhaps the most letter-imperfect of all:

· Mr. & Mrs. Garth Robinson request the honor of your presents at the marriage of their daughter Holly to Mr. James Stockman.

# Howta Reckanize
# Amercan Slurvian

❧

Language lovers have long bewailed the sad state of pronunciation and articulation in the United States. Both in sorrow and in anger, speakers afflicted with sensitive ears wince at such mumblings as *guvmint* for *government* and *assessories* for *accessories.*

Indeed, everywhere we turn we are assaulted by a slew of slurrings. We meet people who *hafta, oughta,* or are *gonna* do something or who *shoulda, woulda,* or *coulda* done it. We hear how they love "drinkin outa bahls" (drinking out of bottles) or how they've "jus been Nittly" (just been in Italy).

Here's a typically American exchange:

"Jeet jet?"

"No, jew?"

. . . Sgo."

Translation: "Did you eat yet?" "No, did you?" "Let's go."

In a 1949 *New Yorker* article, John Davenport

labeled this kind of sublanguage with the delight-
fully appropriate name "Slurvian." Taking
Davenport's lead, H. Alan Wycherley, in *Word Study*,
distinguished between the pure and impure uses of
Slurvian. Impure Slurvian produces nonsense
sounds, such as those I have listed above. But
Slurvian in its purest form mispronounces English
words into *other* English words.

To help you to translate Slurvian into English
and to preserve the growing canon of American
non-enunciation, I offer a grotesque glossary of
pure Slurvian:

*Antidote.* A story. "I love your antidote about the
time you made dinner for the boss."

*Bar.* To take temporarily. "May I bar your
eraser?"

*Calvary.* A mobile army unit. "At the last
minute, the wagon train was saved by the calvary."

*Dense.* A tooth expert. "Yuck! I have a dense
appointment today."

*Forced.* A large cluster of trees. "Only you can
prevent forced fires."

*Formally.* Earlier. "Today she's a millionaire,
but formally she tried to make a living as an English
teacher."

*Forward.* Prefatory remarks by another person.
"Who will write the forward to your book?"

Lays. *The opposite of "gemmen."*

*Girl.* An article of clothing. "She had to work hard to get her girl on."

*Granite.* Conceded. "Too many people take the good life for granite."

*Intensive.* Part of an idiom, as in "for all intensive purposes," rather than the correct "for all intents and purposes."

*Lays.* The opposite of "gemmen." "Lays and gemmen, I now introduce our guest speaker."

*Less.* Contraction of "let us." "Less learn more about Slurvian."

*Lining.* Electrical flash of light. "We abandoned our picnic when we heard the thunder and saw the lining."

*Mayan.* Possessive pronoun. "What's yours is yours, and what's Mayan is Mayan."

*Mere.* A reflecting glass. "Mere, mere on the wall, who's the fairest one of all?"

*Mill.* Between the beginning and the end. "A table stood in the mill of the room."

*Mince.* Unit lasting 60 seconds. "I'll be back in a few mince."

*Money.* Day after Sunny. "I'll be back by next Money."

*Neck Store.* Adjacent. "I'm in love with the girl neck store." A spectacular double play.

*Nigh.* Opposite of day. "She woke up screaming in the mill of the nigh."

*Of.* Have. "I could of danced all nigh."

*Pain.* Giving money. "I'm tired of pain these high prices."

*Pal.* To locomote a craft on water. "It's your turn to pal the canoe."

*Paramour.* A modem grass-cutting instrument. "Less try out the new paramour on the lawn."

*Pitcher.* An image or representation. "As soon as we get the pitcher framed, we'll hang it above the sofa."

*Please.* Officers of the law. "My house was robbed! Call the please!"

*Sunny. Day* before Money. "When Sunny comes, can Money be far behind?"

*Then.* A conjunction. "I like Sunny better then Money."

*Torment. A* competition. "Mabel and I have entered the bridge torment."

*Whore.* Inspiring terror. "I love getting scared out of my pants by whore films."

*Win.* Movement of air. "He was awakened in the mill of the nigh by flashes of lining and gusts of win."

*Winner.* The cold season. "Many birds fly south for the winner."

Slurvophobes unite! Keep your ears open and your notebooks handy, and send me more examples. Together we can record an important second language in the United States and publish a new and useful lexicon—*The Concise Dictionary of American Slurvian.*

# Note

For the more than a thousand examples of anguished English in this book I am deeply indebted to my students, relatives, friends, and hundreds of my readers and listeners who, I trust, will be pleased to find their submissions given national exposure, albeit anonymously or pseudonymously.

To err is human, and to collect verbal error is divine. To those intrepid verbivores who have so divinely gathered bloopers into folk photocopies, books, magazine squibs, and newspaper articles, I offer my profoundest thanks for making this volume more voluminous and hilarious than it otherwise would have been.

*Richard Lederer*